W9-CHH-549

Just The
facts101
Textbook Key Facts

Textbook Outlines, Highlights, and Practice Quizzes

Drugs And Society

by Glen R Hanson, 11th Edition

All "Just the Facts101" Material Written or Prepared by Cram101 Publishing

Title Page

cram101.com

WHY STOP HERE... THERE'S MORE ONLINE

With technology and experience, we've developed tools that make studying easier and efficient. Like this Cram10l textbook notebook, **Cram10l.com** offers you the highlights from every chapter of your actual textbook. However, unlike this notebook, **Cram10l.com** gives you practice tests for each of the chapters. You also get access to in-depth reference material for writing essays and papers.

By purchasing this book, you get 50% off the normal subscription free!. Just enter the promotional code **'DK73DW20957'** on the Cram101.com registration screen.

CRAMl0l.COM FEATURES:

Outlines & Highlights
Just like the ones in this notebook, but with links to additional information.

Integrated Note Taking
Add your class notes to the Cram101 notes, print them and maximize your study time.

Problem Solving
Step-by-step walk throughs for math, stats and other disciplines.

Practice Exams
Five different test taking formats for every chapter.

Easy Access
Study any of your books, on any computer, anywhere.

Unlimited Textbooks
All the features above for virtually all your textbooks, just add them to your account at no additional cost.

Be sure to use the promo code above when registering on Craml0l.com to get 50% off your membership fees.

Visit Cram101.com for full Practice Exams

STUDYING MADE EASY

This Craml0l notebook is designed to make studying easier and increase your comprehension of the textbook material. Instead of starting with a blank notebook and trying to write down everything discussed in class lectures, you can use this Craml0l textbook notebook and annotate your notes along with the lecture.

Our goal is to give you the best tools for success.

For a supreme understanding of the course, pair your notebook with our online tools. Should you decide you prefer Craml0l.com as your study tool,

we'd like to offer you a trade...

Our Trade In program is a simple way for us to keep our promise and provide you the best studying tools, regardless of where you purchased your Craml0l textbook notebook. As long as your notebook is in *Like New Condition**, you can send it back to us and we will immediately give you a Craml0l.com account free for 120 days!

Let The *Trade In* Begin!

THREE SIMPLE STEPS TO TRADE:

1. Go to www.cram101.com/tradein and fill out the packing slip information.

2. Submit and print the packing slip and mail it in with your Craml0l textbook notebook.

3. Activate your account after you receive your email confirmation.

* Books must be returned in *Like New Condition*, meaning there is no damage to the book including, but not limited to; ripped or torn pages, markings or writing on pages, or folded / creased pages. Upon receiving the book, Craml0l will inspect it and reserves the right to terminate your free Craml0l.com account and return your textbook notebook at the owners expense.

Trade-in Program

"Just the Facts101" is a Cram101 publication and tool designed to give you all the facts from your textbooks. Visit Cram101.com for the full practice test for each of your chapters for virtually any of your textbooks.

Cram101 has built custom study tools specific to your textbook. We provide all of the factual testable information and unlike traditional study guides, we will never send you back to your textbook for more information.

YOU WILL NEVER HAVE TO HIGHLIGHT A BOOK AGAIN!

Cram101 StudyGuides

All of the information in this StudyGuide is written specifically for your textbook. We include the key terms, places, people, and concepts... the information you can expect on your next exam!

Want to take a practice test?

Throughout each chapter of this StudyGuide you will find links to cram101.com where you can select specific chapters to take a complete test on, or you can subscribe and get practice tests for up to 12 of your textbooks, along with other exclusive cram101.com tools like problem solving labs and reference libraries.

Cram101.com

Only cram101.com gives you the outlines, highlights, and PRACTICE TESTS specific to your textbook. Cram101.com is an online application where you'll discover study tools designed to make the most of your limited study time.

By purchasing this book, you get 50% off the normal monthly subscription fee!. Just enter the promotional code **'DK73DW20957'** on the Cram101.com registration screen.

www.Cram101.com

Learning System

Drugs And Society
Glen R Hanson, 11th

CONTENTS

CHAPTER OUTLINE: KEY TERMS, PEOPLE, PLACES, CONCEPTS

	Compulsive behavior
	Mental disorder
	Physical dependence
	Substance abuse
	Substance dependence
	Cocaine
	Alcoholics Anonymous
	Narcotics Anonymous
	Personality disorder
	Disordered eating
	Overeaters Anonymous
	Amphetamine
	Benzodiazepine
	Nervous system
	Comorbidity
	Habituation
	Introversion
	Observational learning
	Learning theory

Chapter 1. Explaining Drug Use and Abuse
CHAPTER OUTLINE: KEY TERMS, PEOPLE, PLACES, CONCEPTS

_____ | Social influence

_____ | Significant other

_____ | Social learning theory

_____ | Alcohol abuse

_____ | Demographic profile

_____ | Deviance

_____ | Labeling theory

_____ | Primary deviance

_____ | Secondary deviance

CHAPTER HIGHLIGHTS & NOTES: KEY TERMS, PEOPLE, PLACES, CONCEPTS

Compulsive behavior	Compulsive behavior is defined as performing an act persistently and repetitively without it leading to an actual reward or pleasure. Though compulsive behaviors could be an attempt to make obsessions go away. The act is usually a small, restricted and repetitive behavior, yet not disturbing in a pathological way.
Mental disorder	A mental disorder is a psychological pattern or anomaly, potentially reflected in behavior, that is generally associated with distress or disability, and which is not considered part of normal development of a person's culture. Mental disorders are generally defined by a combination of how a person feels, acts, thinks or perceives. This may be associated with particular regions or functions of the brain or rest of the nervous system, often in a social context.
Physical dependence	Physical dependence refers to a state resulting from chronic use of a drug that has produced tolerance and where negative physical symptoms of withdrawal result from abrupt discontinuation or dosage reduction.

Physical dependence can develop from low-dose therapeutic use of certain medications such as benzodiazepines, opioids, antiepileptics and antidepressants, as well as misuse of recreational drugs such as alcohol, opioids and benzodiazepines. The higher the dose used, the greater the duration of use, and the earlier age use began are predictive of worsened physical dependence and thus more severe withdrawal syndromes.

Substance abuse

Substance abuse, is a patterned use of a substance (drug) in which the user consumes the substance in amounts or with methods neither approved nor supervised by medical professionals. Substance abuse/drug abuse is not limited to mood-altering or psycho-active drugs. If an activity is performed using the objects against the rules and policies of the matter (as in steroids for performance enhancement in sports), it is also called substance abuse.

Substance dependence

Substance dependence, commonly called drug addiction, is a drug user's compulsive need to use controlled substances in order to function normally. When such substances are unobtainable, the user suffers from substance withdrawal.

The section about substance dependence in the Diagnostic and Statistical Manual of Mental Disorders (more specifically, the 2000 'text revision', the DSM-IV-TR) does not use the word addiction at all.

Cocaine

Cocaine benzoylmethylecgonine (INN) is a crystalline tropane alkaloid that is obtained from the leaves of the coca plant. The name comes from 'coca' in addition to the alkaloid suffix -ine, forming cocaine. It is a stimulant of the central nervous system, an appetite suppressant, and a topical anesthetic.

Alcoholics Anonymous

Alcoholics Anonymous is an international mutual aid movement founded in 1935 by Bill Wilson and Dr. Bob Smith (Bill W. and Dr. Bob) in Akron, Ohio. AA states that its 'primary purpose is to stay sober and help other alcoholics achieve sobriety'. With other early members, Wilson and Smith developed AA's Twelve Step program of spiritual and character development.

Narcotics Anonymous

Narcotics Anonymous describes itself as a 'fellowship or society of men and women for whom drugs had become a major problem' following the Twelve Steps and the Twelve Traditions developed by Alcoholics Anonymous, and it is the second-largest 12-step organization.

As of May 2010 there were more than 58,000 NA meetings in 131 countries. Narcotics Anonymous program Membership and organization

The third tradition of NA states that the only requirement for membership is 'a desire to stop using'.

Chapter 1. Explaining Drug Use and Abuse

CHAPTER HIGHLIGHTS & NOTES: KEY TERMS, PEOPLE, PLACES, CONCEPTS

Personality disorder	Personality disorder refers to a class of personality types and enduring behaviors associated with significant distress or disability, which appear to deviate from social expectations particularly in relating to other humans. Personality disorders are included as mental disorders on Axis II of the diagnostic manual of the American Psychiatric Association and in the mental and behavioral disorders section of the ICD manual of the World Health Organization. Personality, defined psychologically, is the set of enduring behavioral and mental traits that distinguish human beings.
Disordered eating	Disordered eating is a classification (within DSM-IV-TR, used in the health-care field) to describe a wide range of irregular eating behaviors that do not warrant a diagnosis of a specific eating disorder such as anorexia nervosa or bulimia nervosa. Affected people may be diagnosed with an eating disorder not otherwise specified. A change in eating patterns can also be caused by other mental disorders (e.g. clinical depression), or by factors that are generally considered to be unrelated to mental disorders (e.g. extreme homesickness).
Overeaters Anonymous	Overeaters Anonymous is a twelve-step program for people with problems related to food including, but not limited to, compulsive overeaters, those with binge eating disorder, bulimics and anorexics. Anyone with a problematic relationship with food is welcomed, as OA's Third Tradition states that the only requirement for memberships is a desire to stop eating compulsively. OA was founded by Rozanne S. and two other women in January 1960. The organization's headquarters, or World Service Office, is located in Rio Rancho, New Mexico.
Amphetamine	Amphetamine or amfetamine (INN) is a psychostimulant drug of the phenethylamine class that is known to produce increased wakefulness and focus in association with decreased fatigue and appetite. Brand names of medications that contain, or metabolize into, amphetamine include Adderall, Dexedrine, Dextrostat, Desoxyn, ProCentra, and Vyvanse, as well as Benzedrine in the past. The drug is also used recreationally and as a performance enhancer.
Benzodiazepine	A benzodiazepine is a psychoactive drug whose core chemical structure is the fusion of a benzene ring and a diazepine ring. The first benzodiazepine, chlordiazepoxide (Librium), was discovered accidentally by Leo Sternbach in 1955, and made available in 1960 by Hoffmann-La Roche, which has also marketed diazepam (Valium) since 1963.
Nervous system	The nervous system is the part of an animal's body that coordinates the actions of the animal and transmits signals between different parts of its body.

Visit Cram101.com for full Practice Exams

	In most types of animals it consists of two main parts, the central nervous system and the peripheral nervous system. The CNS contains the brain and spinal cord.
Comorbidity	In medicine, comorbidity is either the presence of one or more disorders in addition to a primary disease or disorder, or the effect of such additional disorders or diseases. In medicine In medicine, comorbidity describes the effect of all other diseases an individual patient might have other than the primary disease of interest. Many tests attempt to standardize the 'weight' or value of comorbid conditions, whether they are secondary or tertiary illnesses.
Habituation	Habituation, a form of non-associative learning, is the psychological process in humans and other organisms in which there is a decrease in psychological and behavioral response to a stimulus after repeated exposure to that stimulus over a duration of time. Habituation can refer to a decrease in behavior, subjective experience, or synaptic transmission. The changes in synaptic transmission that occur during habituation have been well-characterized in the Aplysia gill and siphon withdrawal reflex.
Introversion	Introversion - a notion introduced by Carl Gustav Jung in the work of Psychologische Typen (Psychological Types, 1921). In psychology, it means a personality trait involving a tendency to drive one's perceptions, actions, thoughts and emotions inside, resulting in reduced interest in activity directed to the outside world.
Observational learning	Observational learning is a type of learning that occurs as a function of observing, retaining and replicating novel behavior executed by others. It is argued that reinforcement has the effect of influencing which responses one will partake in, more than it influences the actual acquisition of the new response.
Learning theory	Learning theories are conceptual frameworks that describe how information is absorbed, processed, and retained during learning. Learning brings together cognitive, emotional, and environmental influences and experiences for acquiring, enhancing, or making changes in one's knowledge, skills, values, and world views. There are three main categories of learning theory: behaviourism, cognitive, and constructivism.
Social influence	Social influence occurs when one's emotions, opinions, or behaviors are affected by others. Social influence takes many forms and can be seen in conformity, socialization, peer pressure, obedience, leadership, persuaon, sales, and marketing.

Chapter 1. Explaining Drug Use and Abuse

Significant other	Significant other is colloquially used as a gender-blind term for a pern's partner in an intimate relationship without disclosing or presuming anything about marital status, relationship status, or sexual orientation, as it is vague enough to avoid offense by using a term that an individual might consider inappropriate (e.g. lover when he considers him a boyfriend, or girlfriend when he considers her a life partner). In the United States the term is metimes used in invitations, e.g., to weddings and office parties. This use of the term has become common in the UK in correspondence from hospitals, e.g., 'you may be accompanied for your appointment by a significant other.' Its usage in both psychology and ciology is very different from its colloquial use.
Social learning theory	Social learning theory is a perspective that states that people learn within a social context. It is facilitated through concepts such as modeling and observational learning. People, especially children, learn from the environment and seek acceptance from society by learning through influential models.
Alcohol abuse	Alcohol abuse, as described in the DSM-IV, is a psychiatric diagnosis describing the recurring use of alcoholic beverages despite its negative consequences. Alcohol abuse is sometimes referred to by the less specific term alcoholism. However, many definitions of alcoholism exist, and only some are compatible with alcohol abuse.
Demographic profile	A demographic profile is a term used in marketing and broadcasting, to describe a demographic grouping or a market segment. This typically involves age bands (as teenagers do not wish to purchase denture fixant), social class bands (as the rich may want different products than middle and lower classes and may be willing to pay more) and gender (partially because different physical attributes require different hygiene and clothing products, and partially because of the male/female mindsets).
Deviance	Deviance in a sociological context describes actions or behaviors that violate cultural norms including formally-enacted rules (e.g., crime) as well as informal violations of social norms (e.g., rejecting folkways and mores). It is the purview of sociologists, psychologists, psychiatrists, and criminologists to study how these norms are created, how they change over time and how they are enforced.
Labeling theory	Labeling theory is closely related to social-construction and symbolic-interaction analysis. Labeling theory was developed by sociologists during the 1960s. Howard Saul Becker's book Outsiders was extremely influential in the development of this theory and its rise to popularity.
Primary deviance	Primary deviance is the first stage in a theory of deviant identity formation. Lemert (1967) conceptualized primary deviance as engaging in the initial act of deviance.

Secondary deviance	Secondary deviance is a stage in a theory of deviant identity formation. Lemert (1967) conceptualized primary deviance as engaging in the initial act of deviance and then posited secondary deviance as the stage in which one internalizes a deviant identity by integrating it into their self-concept.

CHAPTER QUIZ: KEY TERMS, PEOPLE, PLACES, CONCEPTS

1. _____ or amfetamine (INN) is a psychostimulant drug of the phenethylamine class that is known to produce increased wakefulness and focus in association with decreased fatigue and appetite.

Brand names of medications that contain, or metabolize into, _____ include Adderall, Dexedrine, Dextrostat, Desoxyn, ProCentra, and Vyvanse, as well as Benzedrine in the past.

The drug is also used recreationally and as a performance enhancer.

a. Aplindore
b. Amphetamine
c. Azapride
d. Etilevodopa

2. In medicine, _____ is either the presence of one or more disorders in addition to a primary disease or disorder, or the effect of such additional disorders or diseases. In medicine

In medicine, _____ describes the effect of all other diseases an individual patient might have other than the primary disease of interest.

Many tests attempt to standardize the 'weight' or value of comorbid conditions, whether they are secondary or tertiary illnesses.

a. Foerster's syndrome
b. Comorbidity
c. National Mental Health Anti-Stigma Campaign
d. Neuroleptic malignant syndrome

3. . _____ is defined as performing an act persistently and repetitively without it leading to an actual reward or pleasure. Though _____s could be an attempt to make obsessions go away. The act is usually a small, restricted and repetitive behavior, yet not disturbing in a pathological way.

a. Counting method

b. Da Costa's syndrome

c. Compulsive behavior

d. Dermatophagia

4. _____ benzoylmethylecgonine (INN) is a crystalline tropane alkaloid that is obtained from the leaves of the coca plant. The name comes from 'coca' in addition to the alkaloid suffix -ine, forming _____. It is a stimulant of the central nervous system, an appetite suppressant, and a topical anesthetic.

a. Cocaine

b. Cocaine spoon

c. Crack stem

d. D-IX

5. _____, commonly called drug addiction, is a drug user's compulsive need to use controlled substances in order to function normally. When such substances are unobtainable, the user suffers from substance withdrawal.

The section about _____ in the Diagnostic and Statistical Manual of Mental Disorders (more specifically, the 2000 'text revision', the DSM-IV-TR) does not use the word addiction at all.

a. Substance intoxication

b. Substance dependence

c. Traumatic brain injury

d. Trichotillomania

ANSWER KEY
Chapter 1. Explaining Drug Use and Abuse

---

1. b
2. b
3. c
4. a
5. b

You can take the complete Chapter Practice Test

for Chapter 1. Explaining Drug Use and Abuse
on all key terms, persons, places, and concepts.

Online 99 Cents

http://www.epub52.21.20957.1.cram101.com/

Use www.Cram101.com for all your study needs

including Cram101's online interactive problem solving labs in

chemistry, statistics, mathematics, and more.

CHAPTER OUTLINE: KEY TERMS, PEOPLE, PLACES, CONCEPTS

_____ Nervous system

_____ Alcohol advertising

_____ Drug court

_____ Higher Ground

_____ Tobacco

_____ Designer drug

_____ Drug interaction

CHAPTER HIGHLIGHTS & NOTES: KEY TERMS, PEOPLE, PLACES, CONCEPTS

Nervous system	The nervous system is the part of an animal's body that coordinates the actions of the animal and transmits signals between different parts of its body. In most types of animals it consists of two main parts, the central nervous system and the peripheral nervous system. The CNS contains the brain and spinal cord.
Alcohol advertising	Alcohol advertising is the promotion of alcoholic beverages by alcohol producers through a variety of media. Along with tobacco advertising, it is one of the most highly-regulated forms of marketing. Some or all forms of alcohol advertising is banned in some countries.
Drug court	Drug Courts are judicially supervised court dockets that handle the cases of nonviolent substance abusing offenders under the adult, juvenile, family and tribal justice systems. Drug Courts operate under a specialized model in which the judiciary, prosecution, defense bar, probation, law enforcement, mental health, social service, and treatment communities work together to help non-violent offenders find restoration in recovery and become productive citizens. In the USA, there are currently over 2,459 Drug Courts representing all fifty states.
Higher Ground	Higher Ground is a 501(C)3 HIV-AIDS non-profit support group based in Royal Oak, Michigan. Founded in 2002, it primarily serves metropolitan Detroit and southeastern Michigan.

Chapter 2. Drug Use, Regulation, and the Law

Tobacco	Tobacco is an agricultural product processed from the leaves of plants in the genus Nicotiana. It can be consumed, used as an organic pesticide and, in the form of nicotine tartrate, used in some medicines. It is most commonly used as a recreational drug, and is a valuable cash crop for countries such as Cuba, China and the United States.
Designer drug	Designer drug is a term used to describe drugs which are created (or marketed, if they had already existed) to get around existing drug laws, usually by modifying the molecular structures of existing drugs to varying degrees, or less commonly by finding drugs with entirely different chemical structures that produce similar subjective effects to illegal recreational drugs. History United States 1920s-1930s The term 'designer drug' was first coined by law enforcement in the 1980s, and has gained widespread use. However the first appearance of what would now be termed designer drugs occurred well before this, in the 1920s.
Drug interaction	A drug interaction is a situation in which a substance affects the activity of a drug, i.e. the effects are increased or decreased, or they produce a new effect that neither produces on its own. Typically, interaction between drugs come to mind (drug-drug interaction). However, interactions may also exist between drugs & foods (drug-food interactions), as well as drugs & herbs (drug-herb interactions).

1. _____s are judicially supervised court dockets that handle the cases of nonviolent substance abusing offenders under the adult, juvenile, family and tribal justice systems. _____s operate under a specialized model in which the judiciary, prosecution, defense bar, probation, law enforcement, mental health, social service, and treatment communities work together to help non-violent offenders find restoration in recovery and become productive citizens. In the USA, there are currently over 2,459 _____s representing all fifty states.

   a. Drug detoxification
   b. Drug court
   c. Group home
   d. Higher Power

2. The _____ is the part of an animal's body that coordinates the actions of the animal and transmits signals between different parts of its body. In most types of animals it consists of two main parts, the central _____ and the peripheral _____. The CNS contains the brain and spinal cord.

   a. Neural backpropagation
   b. Neural basis of self
   c. Nervous system
   d. Neural decoding

3. _____ is the promotion of alcoholic beverages by alcohol producers through a variety of media. Along with tobacco advertising, it is one of the most highly-regulated forms of marketing. Some or all forms of _____ is banned in some countries.

   a. Approved instrument
   b. Alcohol advertising
   c. Eltham Well Hall rail crash
   d. Ignition interlock device

4. _____ is a 501(C)3 HIV-AIDS non-profit support group based in Royal Oak, Michigan. Founded in 2002, it primarily serves metropolitan Detroit and southeastern Michigan. It frequently receives media coverage for public service.

   a. Hipster PDA
   b. Hoffman Institute
   c. Holland Codes
   d. Higher Ground

5. A _____ is a situation in which a substance affects the activity of a drug, i.e. the effects are increased or decreased, or they produce a new effect that neither produces on its own. Typically, interaction between drugs come to mind (drug-_____). However, interactions may also exist between drugs & foods (drug-food interactions), as well as drugs & herbs (drug-herb interactions).

   a. Drug
   b. Becaplermin
   c. Drug interaction
   d. Biosimilar

1. b
2. c
3. b
4. d
5. c

You can take the complete Chapter Practice Test

for Chapter 2. Drug Use, Regulation, and the Law
on all key terms, persons, places, and concepts.

Online 99 Cents

http://www.epub52.21.20957.2.cram101.com/

Use www.Cram101.com for all your study needs

including Cram101's online interactive problem solving labs in

chemistry, statistics, mathematics, and more.

Chapter 3. Homeostatic Systems and Drugs

CHAPTER OUTLINE: KEY TERMS, PEOPLE, PLACES, CONCEPTS

_____ Anandamide

_____ Amphetamine

_____ Anabolic steroid

_____ Molecular biology

_____ Agonist

_____ Nervous system

_____ Neuron

_____ Depressant

_____ Acetylcholine

_____ Endorphin

_____ Epinephrine

_____ Norepinephrine

_____ Rimonabant

_____ Designer drug

_____ Tobacco

_____ Catecholamine

_____ Reuptake

_____ Tryptophan

_____ Peripheral nervous system

CHAPTER OUTLINE: KEY TERMS, PEOPLE, PLACES, CONCEPTS

	Basal ganglia
	Nucleus accumbens
	Parkinson's disease
	Barbiturate
	Limbic system
	Demographic profile
	Hormone
	Aggression

CHAPTER HIGHLIGHTS & NOTES: KEY TERMS, PEOPLE, PLACES, CONCEPTS

| Anandamide | Anandamide, is an endogenous cannabinoid neurotransmitter. It was isolated and its structure was first described by Czech analytical chemist Lumír Ondrej Hanuš and American molecular pharmacologist William Anthony Devane in 1992. The name is taken from the Sanskrit word ananda, which means 'bliss, delight', and amide. It is synthesized from N-arachidonoyl phosphatidylethanolamine by multiple pathways. It is degraded primarily by the fatty acid amide hydrolase (FAAH) enzyme, which converts anandamide into ethanolamine and arachidonic acid. As such, inhibitors of FAAH lead to elevated anandamide levels and are being pursued for therapeutic use. |
| Amphetamine | Amphetamine or amfetamine (INN) is a psychostimulant drug of the phenethylamine class that is known to produce increased wakefulness and focus in association with decreased fatigue and appetite.

Brand names of medications that contain, or metabolize into, amphetamine include Adderall, Dexedrine, Dextrostat, Desoxyn, ProCentra, and Vyvanse, as well as Benzedrine in the past. |

Chapter 3. Homeostatic Systems and Drugs

Anabolic steroid	Anabolic steroids, technically known as anabolic-androgen steroids, are drugs which mimic the effects of the male sex hormones testosterone and dihydrotestosterone. They increase protein synthesis within cells, which results in the buildup of cellular tissue (anabolism), especially in muscles. Anabolic steroids also have androgenic and virilizing properties, including the development and maintenance of masculine characteristics such as the growth of the vocal cords and body hair.
Molecular biology	Molecular biology is the branch of biology that deals with the molecular basis of biological activity. This field overlaps with other areas of biology and chemistry, particularly genetics and biochemistry. Molecular biology chiefly concerns itself with understanding and the interactions between the various systems of a cell, including the interactions between the different types of DNA, RNA and protein biosynthesis as well as learning how these interactions are regulated.
Agonist	An agonist is a chemical that binds to a receptor of a cell and triggers a response by that cell. Agonists often mimic the action of a naturally occurring substance. Whereas an agonist causes an action, an antagonist blocks the action of the agonist and an inverse agonist causes an action opposite to that of the agonist.
Nervous system	The nervous system is the part of an animal's body that coordinates the actions of the animal and transmits signals between different parts of its body. In most types of animals it consists of two main parts, the central nervous system and the peripheral nervous system. The CNS contains the brain and spinal cord.
Neuron	A neuron is an electrically excitable cell that processes and transmits information by electrical and chemical signaling. Chemical signaling occurs via synapses, specialized connections with other cells. Neurons connect to each other to form networks. Neurons are the core components of the nervous system, which includes the brain, spinal cord, and peripheral ganglia. A number of specialized types of neurons exist: sensory neurons respond to touch, sound, light and numerous other stimuli affecting cells of the sensory organs that then send signals to the spinal cord and brain. Motor neurons receive signals from the brain and spinal cord, cause muscle contractions, and affect glands. Interneurons connect neurons to other neurons within the same region of the brain or spinal cord.
Depressant	A depressant, is a drug or endogenous compound that lowers or depresses arousal levels and reduces excitability. Depressants are also occasionally referred to as 'downers' as they lower the level of arousal when taken. Stimulants or 'uppers' increase mental and/or physical function are the functional opposites of depressants.
Acetylcholine	The chemical compound acetylcholine is a neurotransmitter in both the peripheral nervous system (PNS) and central nervous system (CNS) in many organisms including humans.

Acetylcholine is one of many neurotransmitters in the autonomic nervous system (ANS) and the only neurotransmitter used in the motor division of the somatic nervous system. (Sensory neurons use glutamate and various peptides at their synapses). Acetylcholine is also the principal neurotransmitter in all autonomic ganglia.

Endorphin	Endorphins ('endogenous morphine') are endogenous opioid peptides that function as neurotransmitters. They are produced by the pituitary gland and the hypothalamus in vertebrates during exercise, excitement, pain, consumption of spicy food, love and orgasm, and they resemble the opiates in their abilities to produce analgesia and a feeling of well-being. The term 'endorphin' implies a pharmacological activity (analogous to the activity of the corticosteroid category of biochemicals) as opposed to a specific chemical formulation.
Epinephrine	Epinephrine is a hormone and a neurotransmitter. Epinephrine has many functions in the body, regulating heart rate, blood vessel and air passage diameters, and metabolic shifts; epinephrine release is a crucial component of the fight-or-flight response of the sympathetic nervous system. In chemical terms, epinephrine is one of a group of monoamines called the catecholamines.
Norepinephrine	Norepinephrine is a catecholamine with multiple roles including as a hormone and a neurotransmitter. As a stress hormone, norepinephrine affects parts of the brain, such as the amygdala, where attention and responses are controlled. Along with epinephrine, norepinephrine also underlies the fight-or-flight response, directly increasing heart rate, triggering the release of glucose from energy stores, and increasing blood flow to skeletal muscle. It increases the brain's oxygen supply. Norepinephrine can also suppress neuroinflammation when released diffusely in the brain from the locus ceruleus.
Rimonabant	Rimonabant is an anorectic antiobesity drug that has been withdrawn from the market. It is an inverse agonist for the cannabinoid receptor CB1. Its main effect is reduction in appetite. Rimonabant was the first selective CB1 receptor blocker to be approved for use anywhere in the world.
Designer drug	Designer drug is a term used to describe drugs which are created (or marketed, if they had already existed) to get around existing drug laws, usually by modifying the molecular structures of existing drugs to varying degrees, or less commonly by finding drugs with entirely different chemical structures that produce similar subjective effects to illegal recreational drugs. History

United States

1920s-1930s

The term 'designer drug' was first coined by law enforcement in the 1980s, and has gained widespread use. However the first appearance of what would now be termed designer drugs occurred well before this, in the 1920s.

Tobacco	Tobacco is an agricultural product processed from the leaves of plants in the genus Nicotiana. It can be consumed, used as an organic pesticide and, in the form of nicotine tartrate, used in some medicines. It is most commonly used as a recreational drug, and is a valuable cash crop for countries such as Cuba, China and the United States.
Catecholamine	Catecholamines are 'fight-or-flight' hormones released by the adrenal glands in response to stress. They are part of the sympathetic nervous system. They are called catecholamines because they contain a catechol or 3,4-dihydroxylphenyl group.
Reuptake	Reuptake is the reabsorption of a neurotransmitter by a neurotransmitter transporter of a pre-synaptic neuron after it has performed its function of transmitting a neural impulse. Reuptake is necessary for normal synaptic physiology because it allows for the recycling of neurotransmitters and regulates the level of neurotransmitter present in the synapse and controls how long a signal resulting from neurotransmitter release lasts. Because neurotransmitters are too large and hydrophilic to diffuse through the membrane, specific transport proteins are necessary for the reabsorption of neurotransmitters. Much research, both biochemical and structural, has been performed to obtain clues about the mechanism of reuptake.
Tryptophan	Tryptophan is one of the 20 standard amino acids, as well as an essential amino acid in the human diet. It is encoded in the standard genetic code as the codon UGG. The slight mispronunciation 'tWiptophan' can be used as a mnemonic for its single letter IUPAC code W. Only the L-stereoisomer of tryptophan is used in structural or enzyme proteins, but the D-stereoisomer is occasionally found in naturally produced peptides (for example, the marine venom peptide contryphan). The distinguishing structural characteristic of tryptophan is that it contains an indole functional group.
Peripheral nervous system	The peripheral nervous system consists of the nerves and ganglia outside of the brain and spinal cord. The main function of the Peripheral nervous system is to connect the central nervous system (CNS) to the limbs and organs.

Chapter 3. Homeostatic Systems and Drugs

Basal ganglia	The basal ganglia are a group of nuclei of varied origin in the brains of vertebrates that act as a cohesive functional unit. They are situated at the base of the forebrain and are strongly connected with the cerebral cortex, thalamus and other brain areas. The basal ganglia are associated with a variety of functions, including voluntary motor control, procedural learning relating to routine behaviors or 'habits' such as bruxism, eye movements, and cognitive, emotional functions.
Nucleus accumbens	The nucleus accumbens also known as the accumbens nucleus or as the nucleus accumbens septi, is a collection of neurons within the striatum. It is thought to play an important role in reward, pleasure, laughter, addiction, aggression, fear, and the placebo effect. Each half of the brain has one nucleus accumbens.
Parkinson's disease	Parkinson's disease is a degenerative disorder of the central nervous system. The motor symptoms of Parkinson's disease result from the death of dopamine-generating cells in the substantia nigra, a region of the midbrain; the cause of this cell death is unknown. Early in the course of the disease, the most obvious symptoms are movement-related; these include shaking, rigidity, slowness of movement and difficulty with walking and gait.
Barbiturate	Barbiturates are drugs that act as central nervous system depressants, and, by virtue of this, they produce a wide spectrum of effects, from mild sedation to total anesthesia. They are also effective as anxiolytics, as hypnotics, and as anticonvulsants. They have addiction potential, both physical and psychological.
Limbic system	The limbic system is a complex set of brain structures that lies on both sides of the thalamus, right under the cerebrum. It includes the hippocampus, amygdalae, anterior thalamic nuclei, septum, limbic cortex and fornix, which seemingly support a variety of functions including emotion, behavior, motivation, long-term memory, and olfaction. It appears to be primarily responsible for our emotional life, and has a great deal to do with the formation of memories.
Demographic profile	A demographic profile is a term used in marketing and broadcasting, to describe a demographic grouping or a market segment. This typically involves age bands (as teenagers do not wish to purchase denture fixant), social class bands (as the rich may want different products than middle and lower classes and may be willing to pay more) and gender (partially because different physical attributes require different hygiene and clothing products, and partially because of the male/female mindsets).
Hormone	A hormone is a chemical released by a cell or a gland in one part of the body that sends out messages that affect cells in other parts of the organism. Only a little amount of hormone is required to alter cell metabolism.

Chapter 3. Homeostatic Systems and Drugs

Aggression	Aggression, in its broadest sense, is behavior, or a disposition, that is forceful, hostile or attacking. It may occur either in retaliation or without provocation. In narrower definitions that are used in social sciences and behavioral sciences, aggression is an intention to cause harm or an act intended to increase relative social dominance.

CHAPTER QUIZ: KEY TERMS, PEOPLE, PLACES, CONCEPTS

1. _____, is an endogenous cannabinoid neurotransmitter. It was isolated and its structure was first described by Czech analytical chemist Lumír Ondrej Hanuš and American molecular pharmacologist William Anthony Devane in 1992. The name is taken from the Sanskrit word ananda, which means 'bliss, delight', and amide. It is synthesized from N-arachidonoyl phosphatidylethanolamine by multiple pathways. It is degraded primarily by the fatty acid amide hydrolase (FAAH) enzyme, which converts _____ into ethanolamine and arachidonic acid. As such, inhibitors of FAAH lead to elevated _____ levels and are being pursued for therapeutic use.

   a. Immanuel Kant
   b. Organized Crime Control Act
   c. Anandamide
   d. Abnormal psychology

2. _____ or amfetamine (INN) is a psychostimulant drug of the phenethylamine class that is known to produce increased wakefulness and focus in association with decreased fatigue and appetite.

   Brand names of medications that contain, or metabolize into, _____ include Adderall, Dexedrine, Dextrostat, Desoxyn, ProCentra, and Vyvanse, as well as Benzedrine in the past.

   The drug is also used recreationally and as a performance enhancer.

   a. Aplindore
   b. Amphetamine
   c. Azapride
   d. Etilevodopa

3. . _____ is the reabsorption of a neurotransmitter by a neurotransmitter transporter of a pre-synaptic neuron after it has performed its function of transmitting a neural impulse.

   _____ is necessary for normal synaptic physiology because it allows for the recycling of neurotransmitters and regulates the level of neurotransmitter present in the synapse and controls how long a signal resulting from neurotransmitter release lasts.

Because neurotransmitters are too large and hydrophilic to diffuse through the membrane, specific transport proteins are necessary for the reabsorption of neurotransmitters. Much research, both biochemical and structural, has been performed to obtain clues about the mechanism of _____.

a. Reuptake
b. Norepinephrine
c. Monoamine neurotransmitter
d. Histamine

4. An _____ is a chemical that binds to a receptor of a cell and triggers a response by that cell. _____s often mimic the action of a naturally occurring substance. Whereas an _____ causes an action, an ant_____ blocks the action of the _____ and an inverse _____ causes an action opposite to that of the _____.

a. Agonist
b. Allen's rule
c. Alliesthesia
d. Allometric engineering

5. The chemical compound _____ is a neurotransmitter in both the peripheral nervous system (PNS) and central nervous system (CNS) in many organisms including humans. _____ is one of many neurotransmitters in the autonomic nervous system (ANS) and the only neurotransmitter used in the motor division of the somatic nervous system. (Sensory neurons use glutamate and various peptides at their synapses). _____ is also the principal neurotransmitter in all autonomic ganglia.

a. Immanuel Kant
b. Dieticyclidine
c. Diphenylprolinol
d. Acetylcholine

1. c
2. b
3. a
4. a
5. d

You can take the complete Chapter Practice Test

for Chapter 3. Homeostatic Systems and Drugs
on all key terms, persons, places, and concepts.

Online 99 Cents

http://www.epub52.21.20957.3.cram101.com/

Use www.Cram101.com for all your study needs

including Cram101's online interactive problem solving labs in

chemistry, statistics, mathematics, and more.

Chapter 4. How and Why Drugs Work

CHAPTER OUTLINE: KEY TERMS, PEOPLE, PLACES, CONCEPTS

Cocaine

Side effect

Toxicity

Drug interaction

Hypothetico-deductive model

Nervous system

Blood-brain barrier

Biotransformation

Lactation

Mescaline

Caffeine

Drug metabolism

Alcoholism

Metabolism

Blood test

Testing effect

Reverse tolerance

Craving

Paradoxical reaction

	Physical dependence
	Psychological dependence
	Rebound effect
	Heroin
	Tobacco
	Methadone

CHAPTER HIGHLIGHTS & NOTES: KEY TERMS, PEOPLE, PLACES, CONCEPTS

Cocaine	Cocaine benzoylmethylecgonine (INN) is a crystalline tropane alkaloid that is obtained from the leaves of the coca plant. The name comes from 'coca' in addition to the alkaloid suffix -ine, forming cocaine. It is a stimulant of the central nervous system, an appetite suppressant, and a topical anesthetic.
Side effect	In medicine, a side effect is an effect, whether therapeutic or adverse, that is secondary to the one intended; although the term is predominantly employed to describe adverse effects, it can also apply to beneficial, but unintended, consequences of the use of a drug.

Occasionally, drugs are prescribed or procedures performed specifically for their side effects; in that case, said side effect ceases to be a side effect, and is now an intended effect. For instance, X-rays were historically (and are currently) used as an imaging technique; the discovery of their oncolytic capability led to their employ in radiotherapy (ablation of malignant tumours. |
| Toxicity | Toxicity is the degree to which a substance can damage an organism. Toxicity can refer to the effect on a whole organism, such as an animal, bacterium, or plant, as well as the effect on a substructure of the organism, such as a cell (cytotoxicity) or an organ (organotoxicity), such as the liver (hepatotoxicity). By extension, the word may be metaphorically used to describe toxic effects on larger and more complex groups, such as the family unit or society at large. |
| Drug interaction | A drug interaction is a situation in which a substance affects the activity of a drug, i.e. |

Chapter 4. How and Why Drugs Work

the effects are increased or decreased, or they produce a new effect that neither produces on its own. Typically, interaction between drugs come to mind (drug-drug interaction). However, interactions may also exist between drugs & foods (drug-food interactions), as well as drugs & herbs (drug-herb interactions).

Hypothetico-deductive model	The hypothetico-deductive model, first so-named by William Whewell, is a proposed description of scientific method. According to it, scientific inquiry proceeds by formulating a hypothesis in a form that could conceivably be falsified by a test on observable data. A test that could and does run contrary to predictions of the hypothesis is taken as a falsification of the hypothesis.
Nervous system	The nervous system is the part of an animal's body that coordinates the actions of the animal and transmits signals between different parts of its body. In most types of animals it consists of two main parts, the central nervous system and the peripheral nervous system. The CNS contains the brain and spinal cord.
Blood-brain barrier	The blood-brain barrier is a separation of circulating blood from the brain extracellular fluid (BECF) in the central nervous system (CNS). It occurs along all capillaries and consists of tight junctions around the capillaries that do not exist in normal circulation. Endothelial cells restrict the diffusion of microscopic objects (e.g., bacteria) and large or hydrophilic molecules into the cerebrospinal fluid (CSF), while allowing the diffusion of small hydrophobic molecules (O_2, CO_2, hormones).
Biotransformation	Biotransformation is the chemical modification (or modifications) made by an organism on a chemical compound. If this modification ends in mineral compounds like CO_2, NH_4^+ or H_2O, the biotransformation is called mineralisation. Biotransformation means chemical alteration of chemicals such as (but not limited to) nutrients, amino acids, toxins, or drugs in the body.
Lactation	Lactation describes the secretion of milk from the mammary glands, the process of providing that milk to the young, and the period of time that a mother lactates to feed her young. The process occurs in all female mammals, and in humans it is commonly referred to as breastfeeding or nursing. In most species milk comes out of the mother's nipples; however, the platypus (a non-placental mammal) releases milk through ducts in its abdomen.
Mescaline	Mescaline is a naturally-occurring psychedelic alkaloid of the phenethylamine class used mainly as an entheogen.
	It occurs naturally in the peyote cactus (Lophophora williamsii), the San Pedro cactus (Echinopsis pachanoi) and the Peruvian Torch cactus (Echinopsis peruviana), and in a number of other members of the Cactaceae plant family. It is also found in small amounts in certain members of the Fabaceae (bean) family, including Acacia berlandieri.

Caffeine	Caffeine is a bitter, white crystalline xanthine alkaloid that acts as a stimulant drug. Caffeine is found in varying quantities in the seeds, leaves, and fruit of some plants, where it acts as a natural pesticide that paralyzes and kills certain insects feeding on the plants. It is most commonly consumed by humans in infusions extracted from the seed of the coffee plant and the leaves of the tea bush, as well as from various foods and drinks containing products derived from the kola nut.
Drug metabolism	Drug metabolism is the biochemical modification of pharmaceutical substances by living organisms, usually through specialized enzymatic systems. This is a form of xenobiotic metabolism. Drug metabolism often converts lipophilic chemical compounds into more readily excreted polar products. Its rate is an important determinant of the duration and intensity of the pharmacological action of drugs.
Alcoholism	Alcoholism is a broad term for problems with alcohol, and is generally used to mean compulsive and uncontrolled consumption of alcoholic beverages, usually to the detriment of the drinker's health, personal relationships, and social standing. It is medically considered a disease, specifically an addictive illness, and in psychiatry several other terms are used, specifically 'alcohol abuse' and 'alcohol dependence,' which have slightly different definitions. In 1979 an expert World Health Organization committee discouraged the use of 'alcoholism' in medicine, preferring the category of 'alcohol dependence syndrome'.
Metabolism	Metabolism is the set of chemical reactions that happen in living organisms to maintain life. These processes allow organisms to grow and reproduce, maintain their structures, and respond to their environments. Metabolism is usually divided into two categories. Catabolism breaks down organic matter, for example to harvest energy in cellular respiration. Anabolism uses energy to construct components of cells such as proteins and nucleic acids.
Blood test	A blood test is a laboratory analysis performed on a blood sample that is usually extracted from a vein in the arm using a needle, or via fingerprick. Blood tests are used to determine physiological and biochemical states, such as disease, mineral content, drug effectiveness, and organ function. They are also used in drug tests.
Testing effect	The testing effect refers to the higher probability of recalling an item resulting from the act of retrieving the item from memory (testing) versus additional study trials of the item. However, in order for this effect to be demonstrated the test trials must have a medium to high retrieval success. Logically if the test trials are so difficult that no items are recalled or if the correct answers to the non-recalled items are not given to the test subject, then minimal or no learning will occur.

Chapter 4. How and Why Drugs Work

Reverse tolerance	Reverse tolerance is the phenomenon of a reversal of the side-effects from a drug; the reduction of insensitivity caused after drug tolerance has been established; or, in some cases, an increase in specific effects of a single drug existing alongside a tolerance to the other effects of the same substance.. Typically this involves the use of an additional medication, or abstinence from a drug for a period of time, known as a drug holiday. Such drugs include amphetamines, or SSRIs.
Craving	When going through withdrawal, craving is a psychological urge to administer a discontinued medication or recreational drug. The duration that cravings last after discontinuation varies substantially between different addictive drugs. For instance, in smoking cessation, a substantial relief is achieved after approximately 6-12 months, but feelings of craving may temporarily appear even after many years following cessation.
Paradoxical reaction	A paradoxical reaction is an effect of medical treatment, usually a drug, opposite to the effect which would normally be expected. An example of a paradoxical reaction is when a pain relief medication causes an increase in pain. Some sedatives prescribed for adults actually cause hyperactivity in children.
Physical dependence	Physical dependence refers to a state resulting from chronic use of a drug that has produced tolerance and where negative physical symptoms of withdrawal result from abrupt discontinuation or dosage reduction. Physical dependence can develop from low-dose therapeutic use of certain medications such as benzodiazepines, opioids, antiepileptics and antidepressants, as well as misuse of recreational drugs such as alcohol, opioids and benzodiazepines. The higher the dose used, the greater the duration of use, and the earlier age use began are predictive of worsened physical dependence and thus more severe withdrawal syndromes.
Psychological dependence	In the APA Dictionary of Psychology, psychological dependence is defined as 'dependence on a psychoactive substance for the reinforcement it provides.' Most times psychological dependence is classified under addiction. They are similar in that addiction is a physiological 'craving' for something and psychological dependence is a 'need' for a particular substance because it causes enjoyable mental affects. A person becomes dependent on something to help alleviate specific emotions.
Rebound effect	The rebound effect, is the emergence or re-emergence of symptoms that were either absent or controlled while taking a medication, but appear when that same medication is discontinued, or reduced in dosage.

	In the case of re-emergence, the severity of the symptoms are often worse than pretreatment levels. Examples Sedative hypnotics
	Rebound anxiety
	Several anxiolytics and hypnotics have a rebound effect: For example, benzodiazepine withdrawal can cause severe anxiety and insomnia worse than the original insomnia or anxiety disorder.
Heroin	Heroin (diacetylmorphine (INN)), also known as diamorphine (BAN), is a semi-synthetic opioid drug synthesized from morphine, a derivative of the opium poppy. It is the 3,6-diacetyl ester of morphine (di (two)-acetyl-morphine). The white crystalline form is commonly the hydrochloride salt diacetylmorphine hydrochloride, though often adulterated thus dulling the sheen and consistency from that to a matte white powder, which diacetylmorphine freebase typically is. 90% of diacetylmorphine is thought to be produced in Afghanistan.
Tobacco	Tobacco is an agricultural product processed from the leaves of plants in the genus Nicotiana. It can be consumed, used as an organic pesticide and, in the form of nicotine tartrate, used in some medicines. It is most commonly used as a recreational drug, and is a valuable cash crop for countries such as Cuba, China and the United States.
Methadone	Methadone is a synthetic opioid, used medically as an analgesic and a maintenance anti-addictive for use in patients on opioids. It was developed in Germany in 1937. Although chemically unlike morphine or heroin, methadone also acts on the opioid receptors and thus produces many of the same effects. Methadone is also used in managing chronic pain owing to its long duration of action and very low cost.

CHAPTER QUIZ: KEY TERMS, PEOPLE, PLACES, CONCEPTS

1. . _____ refers to a state resulting from chronic use of a drug that has produced tolerance and where negative physical symptoms of withdrawal result from abrupt discontinuation or dosage reduction. _____ can develop from low-dose therapeutic use of certain medications such as benzodiazepines, opioids, antiepileptics and antidepressants, as well as misuse of recreational drugs such as alcohol, opioids and benzodiazepines. The higher the dose used, the greater the duration of use, and the earlier age use began are predictive of worsened _____ and thus more severe withdrawal syndromes.

    a. Physical dependence
    b. Pragmatic language impairment
    c. Problem gambling

Chapter 4. How and Why Drugs Work

2. A _____ is a situation in which a substance affects the activity of a drug, i.e. the effects are increased or decreased, or they produce a new effect that neither produces on its own. Typically, interaction between drugs come to mind (drug-_____). However, interactions may also exist between drugs & foods (drug-food interactions), as well as drugs & herbs (drug-herb interactions).

   a. Drug interaction
   b. Becaplermin
   c. Biomed 101
   d. Biosimilar

3. _____ is the degree to which a substance can damage an organism. _____ can refer to the effect on a whole organism, such as an animal, bacterium, or plant, as well as the effect on a substructure of the organism, such as a cell (cyto_____) or an organ (organo_____), such as the liver (hepato_____). By extension, the word may be metaphorically used to describe toxic effects on larger and more complex groups, such as the family unit or society at large.

   a. Toxicity
   b. Posse Comitatus Act
   c. Riggins v. Nevada
   d. Therapeutic index

4. _____ is a synthetic opioid, used medically as an analgesic and a maintenance anti-addictive for use in patients on opioids. It was developed in Germany in 1937. Although chemically unlike morphine or heroin, _____ also acts on the opioid receptors and thus produces many of the same effects. _____ is also used in managing chronic pain owing to its long duration of action and very low cost.

   a. Methadone clinic
   b. 18-Methoxycoronaridine
   c. Methadone
   d. Montana Meth Project

5. _____ describes the secretion of milk from the mammary glands, the process of providing that milk to the young, and the period of time that a mother lactates to feed her young. The process occurs in all female mammals, and in humans it is commonly referred to as breastfeeding or nursing. In most species milk comes out of the mother's nipples; however, the platypus (a non-placental mammal) releases milk through ducts in its abdomen.

   a. Lactation
   b. Brain healing
   c. Cerebral blood flow
   d. Cerebral circulation

ANSWER KEY
Chapter 4. How and Why Drugs Work

1. a
2. a
3. a
4. c
5. a

You can take the complete Chapter Practice Test

for Chapter 4. How and Why Drugs Work
on all key terms, persons, places, and concepts.

Online 99 Cents

http://www.epub52.21.20957.4.cram101.com/

Use www.Cram101.com for all your study needs

including Cram101's online interactive problem solving labs in

chemistry, statistics, mathematics, and more.

Chapter 5. CNS Depressants: Sedative-Hypnotics

CHAPTER OUTLINE: KEY TERMS, PEOPLE, PLACES, CONCEPTS

	Cocaine
	Depressant
	Drug interaction
	Nervous system
	Benzodiazepine
	Barbiturate
	Lorazepam
	Triazolam
	Limbic system
	Mescaline
	Paradoxical reaction
	Side effect
	Insomnia
	Benzodiazepine dependence
	Acquaintance rape
	Dextropropoxyphene
	Sexual assault
	Amphetamine
	Chloral hydrate

	Glutethimide
	Methylphenidate
	Methaqualone
	Diphenhydramine
	Hydroxyzine
	Phencyclidine
	Promethazine
	Narcolepsy
	Propofol
	Designer drug
	Datura stramonium

CHAPTER HIGHLIGHTS & NOTES: KEY TERMS, PEOPLE, PLACES, CONCEPTS

Cocaine	Cocaine benzoylmethylecgonine (INN) is a crystalline tropane alkaloid that is obtained from the leaves of the coca plant. The name comes from 'coca' in addition to the alkaloid suffix -ine, forming cocaine. It is a stimulant of the central nervous system, an appetite suppressant, and a topical anesthetic.
Depressant	A depressant, is a drug or endogenous compound that lowers or depresses arousal levels and reduces excitability. Depressants are also occasionally referred to as 'downers' as they lower the level of arousal when taken. Stimulants or 'uppers' increase mental and/or physical function are the functional opposites of depressants.

Drug interaction	A drug interaction is a situation in which a substance affects the activity of a drug, i.e. the effects are increased or decreased, or they produce a new effect that neither produces on its own. Typically, interaction between drugs come to mind (drug-drug interaction). However, interactions may also exist between drugs & foods (drug-food interactions), as well as drugs & herbs (drug-herb interactions).
Nervous system	The nervous system is the part of an animal's body that coordinates the actions of the animal and transmits signals between different parts of its body. In most types of animals it consists of two main parts, the central nervous system and the peripheral nervous system. The CNS contains the brain and spinal cord.
Benzodiazepine	A benzodiazepine is a psychoactive drug whose core chemical structure is the fusion of a benzene ring and a diazepine ring. The first benzodiazepine, chlordiazepoxide (Librium), was discovered accidentally by Leo Sternbach in 1955, and made available in 1960 by Hoffmann-La Roche, which has also marketed diazepam (Valium) since 1963.
Barbiturate	Barbiturates are drugs that act as central nervous system depressants, and, by virtue of this, they produce a wide spectrum of effects, from mild sedation to total anesthesia. They are also effective as anxiolytics, as hypnotics, and as anticonvulsants. They have addiction potential, both physical and psychological.
Lorazepam	Lorazepam is an high potency short to intermediate acting 3-hydroxy benzodiazepine drug which has all five intrinsic benzodiazepine effects: anxiolytic, amnesic, sedative/hypnotic, anticonvulsant and muscle relaxant. Lorazepam is used for the short-term treatment of anxiety, insomnia, acute seizures including status epilepticus and sedation of hospitalised patients, as well as sedation of aggressive patients.
Triazolam	Triazolam is a benzodiazepine derivative drug. It possesses pharmacological properties similar to that of other benzodiazepines, but it is generally only used as a sedative to treat severe insomnia. In addition to the hypnotic properties triazolam possesses, amnesic, anxiolytic, sedative, anticonvulsant and muscle relaxant properties are also present. Due to its short half-life, triazolam is not effective for patients that suffer from frequent awakenings or early wakening.
Limbic system	The limbic system is a complex set of brain structures that lies on both sides of the thalamus, right under the cerebrum. It includes the hippocampus, amygdalae, anterior thalamic nuclei, septum, limbic cortex and fornix, which seemingly support a variety of functions including emotion, behavior, motivation, long-term memory, and olfaction. It appears to be primarily responsible for our emotional life, and has a great deal to do with the formation of memories.
Mescaline	Mescaline is a naturally-occurring psychedelic alkaloid of the phenethylamine class used mainly as an entheogen.

Chapter 5. CNS Depressants: Sedative-Hypnotics

It occurs naturally in the peyote cactus (Lophophora williamsii), the San Pedro cactus (Echinopsis pachanoi) and the Peruvian Torch cactus (Echinopsis peruviana), and in a number of other members of the Cactaceae plant family. It is also found in small amounts in certain members of the Fabaceae (bean) family, including Acacia berlandieri.

Paradoxical reaction

A paradoxical reaction is an effect of medical treatment, usually a drug, opposite to the effect which would normally be expected.

An example of a paradoxical reaction is when a pain relief medication causes an increase in pain. Some sedatives prescribed for adults actually cause hyperactivity in children.

Side effect

In medicine, a side effect is an effect, whether therapeutic or adverse, that is secondary to the one intended; although the term is predominantly employed to describe adverse effects, it can also apply to beneficial, but unintended, consequences of the use of a drug.

Occasionally, drugs are prescribed or procedures performed specifically for their side effects; in that case, said side effect ceases to be a side effect, and is now an intended effect. For instance, X-rays were historically (and are currently) used as an imaging technique; the discovery of their oncolytic capability led to their employ in radiotherapy (ablation of malignant tumours.

Insomnia

Insomnia, is a sleep disorder in which there is an inability to fall asleep or to stay asleep as long as desired. While the term is sometimes used to describe a disorder demonstrated by polysomnographic evidence of disturbed sleep, insomnia is often practically defined as a positive response to either of two questions: 'Do you experience difficulty sleeping?' or 'Do you have difficulty falling or staying asleep?'

Thus, insomnia is most often thought of as both a sign and a symptom that can accompany several sleep, medical, and psychiatric disorders characterized by a persistent difficulty falling asleep and/or staying asleep or sleep of poor quality. Insomnia is typically followed by functional impairment while awake.

Benzodiazepine dependence

Benzodiazepine dependence is when one has developed three or more of either tolerance, withdrawal symptoms, drug seeking behaviors, continued use despite harmful effects, and maladaptive pattern of substance use, according to the DSM-IV. In the case of benzodizepine dependence however, the continued use seems to be associated with the avoidance of unpleasant withdrawal reaction rather than from the pleasurable effects of the drug. Benzodiazepine dependence develops with long term use, even at low therapeutic doses, even without the described dependence behavior.

Acquaintance rape	Acquaintance rape is an assault or attempted assault usually committed by a new acquaintance involving sexual intercourse without mutual consent.
	The term 'date rape' is widely used but can be misleading because the person who commits the crime might not be dating the victim. Rather, it could be an acquaintance or stranger.
Dextropropoxyphene	Dextropropoxyphene, manufactured by Eli Lilly and Company, is an analgesic in the opioid category. It is intended to to treat mild pain and has, in addition, anti-tussive and local anesthetic effects. It has been taken off the marked in Europe and the US due to concerns of fatal overdoses and arrhythmias.
Sexual assault	Sexual assault is an assault of a sexual nature on another person, or any sexual act committed without consent. Although sexual assaults most frequently are by a man on a woman, it may involve any combination of two or more men, women and children.
	The term sexual assault is used, in public discourse, as a generic term that is defined as any involuntary sexual act in which a person is threatened, coerced, or forced to engage against their will, or any sexual touching of a person who has not consented.
Amphetamine	Amphetamine or amfetamine (INN) is a psychostimulant drug of the phenethylamine class that is known to produce increased wakefulness and focus in association with decreased fatigue and appetite.
	Brand names of medications that contain, or metabolize into, amphetamine include Adderall, Dexedrine, Dextrostat, Desoxyn, ProCentra, and Vyvanse, as well as Benzedrine in the past.
	The drug is also used recreationally and as a performance enhancer.
Chloral hydrate	Chloral hydrate is a sedative and hypnotic drug as well as a chemical reagent and precursor. The name chloral hydrate indicates that it is formed from chloral (trichloroacetaldehyde) by the addition of one molecule of water. Its chemical formula is $C_2H_3Cl_3O_2$.
Glutethimide	Glutethimide is a hypnotic sedative that was introduced in 1954 as a safe alternative to barbiturates to treat insomnia. Before long, however, it had become clear that glutethimide was just as likely to cause addiction and caused similarly severe withdrawal symptoms. Doriden is the brand-name version of the drug; both the generic and brand-name forms are rarely prescribed today.
Methylphenidate	Methylphenidate is a psychostimulant drug approved for treatment of attention-deficit hyperactivity disorder, postural orthostatic tachycardia syndrome, and narcolepsy.

It may also be prescribed for off-label use in treatment-resistant cases of lethargy, depression, neural insult and obesity.

Methylphenidate belongs to the piperidine class of compounds and increases the levels of dopamine and norepinephrine in the brain through reuptake inhibition of the monoamine transporters.

Methaqualone	Methaqualone is a sedative-hypnotic drug that is similar in effect to barbiturates, a general central nervous system depressant. Its use peaked in the 1960s and 1970s as a hypnotic, for the treatment of insomnia, and as a sedative and muscle relaxant. It has also been used illegally as a recreational drug, commonly known as Quaaludes, Sopors, Ludes or Mandrax (particularly in the 1970s in North America/Canada) depending on the manufacturer.
Diphenhydramine	Diphenhydramine hydrochloride is a first generation antihistamine mainly used to treat allergies. Like most other first generation antihistamines, the drug also has a powerful hypnotic effect, and for this reason is often used as a nonprescription sleep aid and a mild anxiolytic. The drug also acts as an antiemetic.
Hydroxyzine	Hydroxyzine is a first-generation antihistamine of the diphenylmethane and piperazine classes. It was first synthesized by Union Chimique Belge in 1956 and was marketed by Pfizer in the United States later the same year, and is still in widespread use today. Hydroxyzine is used primarily as an antihistamine for the treatment of itching, allergies, hyperalgesia, motion sickness-induced nausea, and insomnia, as well as notably for the treatment of mild anxiety.
Phencyclidine	Phencyclidine (a complex clip of the chemical name 1-(1-phenylcyclohexyl)piperidine, commonly initialized as PCP), also known as angel dust and myriad other street names, is a recreational, dissociative drug formerly used as an anesthetic agent, exhibiting hallucinogenic and neurotoxic effects. Developed in 1926, it was first patented in 1952 by the Parke-Davis pharmaceutical company and marketed under the brand name Sernyl. In chemical structure, PCP is an arylcyclohexylamine derivative, and, in pharmacology, it is a member of the family of dissociative anesthetics. PCP works primarily as an NMDA receptor antagonist, which blocks the activity of the NMDA receptor and, like most antiglutamatergic hallucinogens, is significantly more dangerous than other categories of hallucinogens. Other NMDA receptor antagonists include ketamine, tiletamine, and dextromethorphan. Although the primary psychoactive effects of the drug lasts for a few hours, the total elimination rate from the body typically extends eight days or longer.

Promethazine	Promethazine is a first-generation H_1 receptor antagonist of the phenothiazine chemical class used medically as an antihistamine antiemetic. It has a strong sedative effect and in some countries is prescribed for insomnia when benzodiazepines are contraindicated. It is available over the counter in the United Kingdom, Australia, Switzerland, and many other countries, but by prescription in the United States (brand names Phenergan, Promethegan, Romergan, Fargan, Farganesse, Prothiazine, Avomine, Atosil, Receptozine, Lergigan).
Narcolepsy	Narcolepsy is a chronic neurological disorder caused by the brain's inability to regulate sleep-wake cycles normally. People with narcolepsy often experience disturbed nocturnal sleep and an abnormal daytime sleep pattern, which often is confused with insomnia. Narcoleptics, when falling asleep, generally experience the REM stage of sleep within 5 minutes, while most people do not experience REM sleep until an hour or so later.
Propofol	Propofol is a short-acting, intravenously administered hypnotic agent. Its uses include the induction and maintenance of general anesthesia, sedation for mechanically ventilated adults, and procedural sedation.
Designer drug	Designer drug is a term used to describe drugs which are created (or marketed, if they had already existed) to get around existing drug laws, usually by modifying the molecular structures of existing drugs to varying degrees, or less commonly by finding drugs with entirely different chemical structures that produce similar subjective effects to illegal recreational drugs. History United States 1920s-1930s The term 'designer drug' was first coined by law enforcement in the 1980s, and has gained widespread use. However the first appearance of what would now be termed designer drugs occurred well before this, in the 1920s.
Datura stramonium	Datura stramonium It is an erect annual herb forming a bush up to 3-5 ft (1-1.5 m) tall. The leaves are soft, irregularly undulate, and toothed. The fragrant flowers are trumpet-shaped, white to creamy or violet, and 2.5 to 3.5 in. long. They rarely open completely. The egg-shaped seed capsule is walnut-sized and either covered with spines or bald. At maturity it splits into four chambers, each with dozens of small black seeds.Parts of the plant, especially the seeds and leaves, are sometimes used as a hallucinogen. Due to the elevated risk of overdose in uninformed users, many hospitalizations, and some deaths, are reported from this use.

Chapter 5. CNS Depressants: Sedative-Hypnotics

1. The _____ is the part of an animal's body that coordinates the actions of the animal and transmits signals between different parts of its body. In most types of animals it consists of two main parts, the central _____ and the peripheral _____. The CNS contains the brain and spinal cord.

   a. Neural backpropagation
   b. Nervous system
   c. Neural coding
   d. Neural decoding

2. A _____ is a situation in which a substance affects the activity of a drug, i.e. the effects are increased or decreased, or they produce a new effect that neither produces on its own. Typically, interaction between drugs come to mind (drug-_____). However, interactions may also exist between drugs & foods (drug-food interactions), as well as drugs & herbs (drug-herb interactions).

   a. Drug
   b. Becaplermin
   c. Biomed 101
   d. Drug interaction

3. _____ is an high potency short to intermediate acting 3-hydroxy benzodiazepine drug which has all five intrinsic benzodiazepine effects: anxiolytic, amnesic, sedative/hypnotic, anticonvulsant and muscle relaxant. _____ is used for the short-term treatment of anxiety, insomnia, acute seizures including status epilepticus and sedation of hospitalised patients, as well as sedation of aggressive patients.

   a. Prochlorperazine
   b. Lorazepam
   c. Chlorpromazine
   d. Prazepam

4. _____ is a sedative and hypnotic drug as well as a chemical reagent and precursor. The name _____ indicates that it is formed from chloral (trichloroacetaldehyde) by the addition of one molecule of water. Its chemical formula is $C_2H_3Cl_3O_2$.

   a. Chloralodol
   b. Chlorobutanol
   c. Clomethiazole
   d. Chloral hydrate

5. . A _____ is a psychoactive drug whose core chemical structure is the fusion of a benzene ring and a diazepine ring. The first _____, chlordiazepoxide (Librium), was discovered accidentally by Leo Sternbach in 1955, and made available in 1960 by Hoffmann-La Roche, which has also marketed diazepam (Valium) since 1963.

   a. Benzodiazepine
   b. Neural basis of self

c. Neural coding

d. Neural decoding

1. b
2. d
3. b
4. d
5. a

You can take the complete Chapter Practice Test

for Chapter 5. CNS Depressants: Sedative-Hypnotics
on all key terms, persons, places, and concepts.

Online 99 Cents

http://www.epub52.21.20957.5.cram101.com/

Use www.Cram101.com for all your study needs

including Cram101's online interactive problem solving labs in

chemistry, statistics, mathematics, and more.

Side effect

Ethanol

Methaqualone

Sexual assault

Alcohol dehydrogenase

Alcohol tolerance

Metabolism

Disinhibition

Hangover

Hormone

Disulfiram

Naltrexone

Alcohol dependence

Alcoholics Anonymous

Nervous system

Agonist

Alcohol abuse

Endorphin

Alcoholic hepatitis

Chapter 6. Alcohol: Pharmacological Effects
CHAPTER OUTLINE: KEY TERMS, PEOPLE, PLACES, CONCEPTS

	Fetal alcohol syndrome
	Mental disorder

CHAPTER HIGHLIGHTS & NOTES: KEY TERMS, PEOPLE, PLACES, CONCEPTS

Side effect	In medicine, a side effect is an effect, whether therapeutic or adverse, that is secondary to the one intended; although the term is predominantly employed to describe adverse effects, it can also apply to beneficial, but unintended, consequences of the use of a drug. Occasionally, drugs are prescribed or procedures performed specifically for their side effects; in that case, said side effect ceases to be a side effect, and is now an intended effect. For instance, X-rays were historically (and are currently) used as an imaging technique; the discovery of their oncolytic capability led to their employ in radiotherapy (ablation of malignant tumours.
Ethanol	Ethanol, pure alcohol, grain alcohol, or drinking alcohol, is a volatile, flammable, colorless liquid. It is a powerful psychoactive drug and one of the oldest recreational drugs. Best known as the type of alcohol found in alcoholic beverages, it is also used in thermometers, as a solvent, and as an alcohol fuel.
Methaqualone	Methaqualone is a sedative-hypnotic drug that is similar in effect to barbiturates, a general central nervous system depressant. Its use peaked in the 1960s and 1970s as a hypnotic, for the treatment of insomnia, and as a sedative and muscle relaxant. It has also been used illegally as a recreational drug, commonly known as Quaaludes, Sopors, Ludes or Mandrax (particularly in the 1970s in North America/Canada) depending on the manufacturer.
Sexual assault	Sexual assault is an assault of a sexual nature on another person, or any sexual act committed without consent. Although sexual assaults most frequently are by a man on a woman, it may involve any combination of two or more men, women and children. The term sexual assault is used, in public discourse, as a generic term that is defined as any involuntary sexual act in which a person is threatened, coerced, or forced to engage against their will, or any sexual touching of a person who has not consented.

Alcohol dehydrogenase	Alcohol dehydrogenases (ADH) (EC 1.1.1.1) are a group of dehydrogenase enzymes that occur in many organisms and facilitate the interconversion between alcohols and aldehydes or ketones with the reduction of nicotinamide adenine dinucleotide (NAD^+ to NADH). In humans and many other animals, they serve to break down alcohols that otherwise are toxic, and they also participate in generation of useful aldehyde, ketone, or alcohol groups during biosynthesis of various metabolites. In yeast, plants, and many bacteria, some alcohol dehydrogenases catalyze the opposite reaction as part of fermentation to ensure a constant supply of NAD^+.
Alcohol tolerance	Alcohol tolerance refers to the bodily responses to the functional effects of ethanol in alcoholic beverages. This includes direct tolerance, speed of recovery from insobriety and resistance to the development of alcoholism. Consumption-induced tolerance Alcohol tolerance is increased by regular drinking.
Metabolism	Metabolism is the set of chemical reactions that happen in living organisms to maintain life. These processes allow organisms to grow and reproduce, maintain their structures, and respond to their environments. Metabolism is usually divided into two categories. Catabolism breaks down organic matter, for example to harvest energy in cellular respiration. Anabolism uses energy to construct components of cells such as proteins and nucleic acids.
Disinhibition	In psychology, disinhibition is a lack of restraint manifested in several ways, including disregard for social conventions, impulsivity, and poor risk assessment. Disinhibition affects motor, instinctual, emotional, cognitive, and perceptual aspects with signs and symptoms similar to the diagnostic criteria for mania. Hypersexuality, hyperphagia, and aggressive outbursts are indicative of disinhibited instinctual drives.
Hangover	A hangover pron.: (medical terminology: veisalgia) is the experience of various unpleasant physiological effects following heavy consumption of alcoholic beverages. The most commonly reported characteristics of a hangover include headache, nausea, sensitivity to light and noise, lethargy, dysphoria, diarrhea and thirst, typically after the intoxicating effect of the alcohol begins to wear off. While a hangover can be experienced at any time, generally a hangover is experienced the morning after a night of heavy drinking.
Hormone	A hormone is a chemical released by a cell or a gland in one part of the body that sends out messages that affect cells in other parts of the organism. Only a little amount of hormone is required to alter cell metabolism. In essence, it is a chemical messenger that transports a signal from one cell to another.

Chapter 6. Alcohol: Pharmacological Effects

Disulfiram	Disulfiram is a drug discovered in the 1920s and used to support the treatment of chronic alcoholism by producing an acute sensitivity to alcohol. It blocks the processing of alcohol in the body by inhibiting acetaldehyde dehydrogenase thus causing an unpleasant reaction when alcohol is consumed. Disulfiram should be used in conjunction with counseling and support.
Naltrexone	Naltrexone is an opioid receptor antagonist used primarily in the management of alcohol dependence and opioid dependence. It is marketed in generic form as its hydrochloride salt, naltrexone hydrochloride, and marketed under the trade names Revia and Depade. In some countries including the United States, a once-monthly extended-release injectable formulation is marketed under the trade name Vivitrol.
Alcohol dependence	Alcohol dependence is a substance related disorder in which an individual is addicted to alcohol either physically or mentally, and continues to use alcohol despite significant areas of dysfunction, evidence of physical dependence, and/or related hardship. Definition and diagnosis According to the DSM-IV criteria for alcohol dependence, at least three out of seven of the following criteria must be manifest during a 12 month period:•Tolerance•Withdrawal symptoms or clinically defined Alcohol Withdrawal Syndrome•Use in larger amounts or for longer periods than intended•Persistent desire or unsuccessful efforts to cut down on alcohol use•Time is spent obtaining alcohol or recovering from effects•Social, occupational and recreational pursuits are given up or reduced because of alcohol use•Use is continued despite knowledge of alcohol-related harm (physical or psychological) History and epidemiology About 12% of American adults have had an alcohol dependence problem at some time in their life. The term 'alcohol dependence' has replaced 'alcoholism' as a term in order that individuals do not internalize the idea of cure and disease, but can approach alcohol as a chemical they may depend upon to cope with outside pressures.
Alcoholics Anonymous	Alcoholics Anonymous is an international mutual aid movement founded in 1935 by Bill Wilson and Dr. Bob Smith (Bill W. and Dr. Bob) in Akron, Ohio. AA states that its 'primary purpose is to stay sober and help other alcoholics achieve sobriety'. With other early members, Wilson and Smith developed AA's Twelve Step program of spiritual and character development.
Nervous system	The nervous system is the part of an animal's body that coordinates the actions of the animal and transmits signals between different parts of its body. In most types of animals it consists of two main parts, the central nervous system and the peripheral nervous system. The CNS contains the brain and spinal cord.
Agonist	An agonist is a chemical that binds to a receptor of a cell and triggers a response by that cell. Agonists often mimic the action of a naturally occurring substance.

Alcohol abuse	Alcohol abuse, as described in the DSM-IV, is a psychiatric diagnosis describing the recurring use of alcoholic beverages despite its negative consequences. Alcohol abuse is sometimes referred to by the less specific term alcoholism. However, many definitions of alcoholism exist, and only some are compatible with alcohol abuse.
Endorphin	Endorphins ('endogenous morphine') are endogenous opioid peptides that function as neurotransmitters. They are produced by the pituitary gland and the hypothalamus in vertebrates during exercise, excitement, pain, consumption of spicy food, love and orgasm, and they resemble the opiates in their abilities to produce analgesia and a feeling of well-being. The term 'endorphin' implies a pharmacological activity (analogous to the activity of the corticosteroid category of biochemicals) as opposed to a specific chemical formulation.
Alcoholic hepatitis	Alcoholic hepatitis is hepatitis (inflammation of the liver) due to excessive intake of alcohol. It is usually found in association with hepatosteatosis, an early stage of alcoholic liver disease, and may contribute to the progression of fibrosis, leading to cirrhosis . Symptoms are jaundice, ascites (fluid accumulation in the abdominal cavity), fatigue and hepatic encephalopathy (brain dysfunction due to liver failure).
Fetal alcohol syndrome	Fetal alcohol syndrome is a pattern of mental and physical defects that can develop in a fetus in association with high levels of alcohol consumption during pregnancy. Current research also implicates other lifestyle choices made by the prospective mother. Indications for lower levels of alcohol are inconclusive.
Mental disorder	A mental disorder is a psychological pattern or anomaly, potentially reflected in behavior, that is generally associated with distress or disability, and which is not considered part of normal development of a person's culture. Mental disorders are generally defined by a combination of how a person feels, acts, thinks or perceives. This may be associated with particular regions or functions of the brain or rest of the nervous system, often in a social context.

Chapter 6. Alcohol: Pharmacological Effects

1. The _____ is the part of an animal's body that coordinates the actions of the animal and transmits signals between different parts of its body. In most types of animals it consists of two main parts, the central _____ and the peripheral _____. The CNS contains the brain and spinal cord.

   a. Nervous system
   b. Neural basis of self
   c. Neural coding
   d. Neural decoding

2. An _____ is a chemical that binds to a receptor of a cell and triggers a response by that cell. _____s often mimic the action of a naturally occurring substance. Whereas an _____ causes an action, an ant_____ blocks the action of the _____ and an inverse _____ causes an action opposite to that of the _____.

   a. Aldosterone escape
   b. Agonist
   c. Alliesthesia
   d. Allometric engineering

3. _____, pure alcohol, grain alcohol, or drinking alcohol, is a volatile, flammable, colorless liquid. It is a powerful psychoactive drug and one of the oldest recreational drugs. Best known as the type of alcohol found in alcoholic beverages, it is also used in thermometers, as a solvent, and as an alcohol fuel.

   a. Etifoxine
   b. ICI-190,622
   c. Ethanol
   d. Ipsapirone

4. . _____ is a substance related disorder in which an individual is addicted to alcohol either physically or mentally, and continues to use alcohol despite significant areas of dysfunction, evidence of physical dependence, and/or related hardship. Definition and diagnosis

   According to the DSM-IV criteria for _____, at least three out of seven of the following criteria must be manifest during a 12 month period:•Tolerance•Withdrawal symptoms or clinically defined Alcohol Withdrawal Syndrome•Use in larger amounts or for longer periods than intended•Persistent desire or unsuccessful efforts to cut down on alcohol use•Time is spent obtaining alcohol or recovering from effects•Social, occupational and recreational pursuits are given up or reduced because of alcohol use•Use is continued despite knowledge of alcohol-related harm (physical or psychological) History and epidemiology

   About 12% of American adults have had an _____ problem at some time in their life. The term '_____' has replaced 'alcoholism' as a term in order that individuals do not internalize the idea of cure and disease, but can approach alcohol as a chemical they may depend upon to cope with outside pressures.

   a. Alcohol detoxification

b. Alcohol dependence

c. Alcohol enema

d. Alcohol intoxication

5. _____ is a sedative-hypnotic drug that is similar in effect to barbiturates, a general central nervous system depressant. Its use peaked in the 1960s and 1970s as a hypnotic, for the treatment of insomnia, and as a sedative and muscle relaxant. It has also been used illegally as a recreational drug, commonly known as Quaaludes, Sopors, Ludes or Mandrax (particularly in the 1970s in North America/Canada) depending on the manufacturer.

a. 2-Methyl-2-butanol

b. Methaqualone

c. Methylmethaqualone

d. Minitran

1. a
2. b
3. c
4. b
5. b

You can take the complete Chapter Practice Test

for Chapter 6. Alcohol: Pharmacological Effects
on all key terms, persons, places, and concepts.

Online 99 Cents

http://www.epub52.21.20957.6.cram101.com/

Use www.Cram101.com for all your study needs

including Cram101's online interactive problem solving labs in

chemistry, statistics, mathematics, and more.

_____ Alcohol abuse

_____ Alcoholism

_____ Heroin

_____ Alcohol dependence

_____ Alcohol tolerance

_____ Disinhibition

_____ Alcoholics Anonymous

_____ Sexual assault

_____ Binge drinking

_____ Domestic violence

_____ Physical abuse

_____ Acquaintance rape

_____ Codependency

_____ Enabling

_____ Adult Children of Alcoholics

_____ Delirium tremens

_____ Disulfiram

_____ Naltrexone

_____ Genogram

| | Psychodrama |

| Alcohol abuse | Alcohol abuse, as described in the DSM-IV, is a psychiatric diagnosis describing the recurring use of alcoholic beverages despite its negative consequences. Alcohol abuse is sometimes referred to by the less specific term alcoholism. However, many definitions of alcoholism exist, and only some are compatible with alcohol abuse. |

| Alcoholism | Alcoholism is a broad term for problems with alcohol, and is generally used to mean compulsive and uncontrolled consumption of alcoholic beverages, usually to the detriment of the drinker's health, personal relationships, and social standing. It is medically considered a disease, specifically an addictive illness, and in psychiatry several other terms are used, specifically 'alcohol abuse' and 'alcohol dependence,' which have slightly different definitions. In 1979 an expert World Health Organization committee discouraged the use of 'alcoholism' in medicine, preferring the category of 'alcohol dependence syndrome'. |

| Heroin | Heroin (diacetylmorphine (INN)), also known as diamorphine (BAN), is a semi-synthetic opioid drug synthesized from morphine, a derivative of the opium poppy. It is the 3,6-diacetyl ester of morphine (di (two)-acetyl-morphine). The white crystalline form is commonly the hydrochloride salt diacetylmorphine hydrochloride, though often adulterated thus dulling the sheen and consistency from that to a matte white powder, which diacetylmorphine freebase typically is. 90% of diacetylmorphine is thought to be produced in Afghanistan. |

| Alcohol dependence | Alcohol dependence is a substance related disorder in which an individual is addicted to alcohol either physically or mentally, and continues to use alcohol despite significant areas of dysfunction, evidence of physical dependence, and/or related hardship. Definition and diagnosis

According to the DSM-IV criteria for alcohol dependence, at least three out of seven of the following criteria must be manifest during a 12 month period:•Tolerance•Withdrawal symptoms or clinically defined Alcohol Withdrawal Syndrome•Use in larger amounts or for longer periods than intended•Persistent desire or unsuccessful efforts to cut down on alcohol use•Time is spent obtaining alcohol or recovering from effects•Social, occupational and recreational pursuits are given up or reduced because of alcohol use•Use is continued despite knowledge of alcohol-related harm (physical or psychological) History and epidemiology |

About 12% of American adults have had an alcohol dependence problem at some time in their life. The term 'alcohol dependence' has replaced 'alcoholism' as a term in order that individuals do not internalize the idea of cure and disease, but can approach alcohol as a chemical they may depend upon to cope with outside pressures.

Alcohol tolerance	Alcohol tolerance refers to the bodily responses to the functional effects of ethanol in alcoholic beverages. This includes direct tolerance, speed of recovery from insobriety and resistance to the development of alcoholism. Consumption-induced tolerance Alcohol tolerance is increased by regular drinking.
Disinhibition	In psychology, disinhibition is a lack of restraint manifested in several ways, including disregard for social conventions, impulsivity, and poor risk assessment. Disinhibition affects motor, instinctual, emotional, cognitive, and perceptual aspects with signs and symptoms similar to the diagnostic criteria for mania. Hypersexuality, hyperphagia, and aggressive outbursts are indicative of disinhibited instinctual drives.
Alcoholics Anonymous	Alcoholics Anonymous is an international mutual aid movement founded in 1935 by Bill Wilson and Dr. Bob Smith (Bill W. and Dr. Bob) in Akron, Ohio. AA states that its 'primary purpose is to stay sober and help other alcoholics achieve sobriety'. With other early members, Wilson and Smith developed AA's Twelve Step program of spiritual and character development.
Sexual assault	Sexual assault is an assault of a sexual nature on another person, or any sexual act committed without consent. Although sexual assaults most frequently are by a man on a woman, it may involve any combination of two or more men, women and children. The term sexual assault is used, in public discourse, as a generic term that is defined as any involuntary sexual act in which a person is threatened, coerced, or forced to engage against their will, or any sexual touching of a person who has not consented.
Binge drinking	Binge drinking is the modern epithet for drinking alcoholic beverages with the primary intention of becoming intoxicated by heavy consumption of alcohol over a short period of time. It is a kind of purposeful drinking style that is popular in several countries worldwide, and overlaps somewhat with social drinking since it is often done in groups. The degree of intoxication, however, varies between and within various cultures that engage in this practice.

Chapter 7. Alcohol: Behavioral Effects

Domestic violence	Domestic violence, spousal abuse, battering, family violence, and intimate partner violence (IPV), is defined as a pattern of abusive behaviors by one partner against another in an intimate relationship such as marriage, dating, family, or cohabitation. Domestic violence, so defined, has many forms, including physical aggression or assault (hitting, kicking, biting, shoving, restraining, slapping, throwing objects), or threats thereof; sexual abuse; emotional abuse; controlling or domineering; intimidation; stalking; passive/covert abuse (e.g., neglect); and economic deprivation. Alcohol consumption and mental illness can be co-morbid with abuse, and present additional challenges in eliminating domestic violence.
Physical abuse	Physical abuse is an act of another party involving contact intended to cause feelings of physical pain, injury, or other physical suffering or bodily harm. Physical abuse has been described among animals too, for example among the Adélie penguins. In most cases, children are the victims of physical abuse, but adults can be the sufferers too.
Acquaintance rape	Acquaintance rape is an assault or attempted assault usually committed by a new acquaintance involving sexual intercourse without mutual consent. The term 'date rape' is widely used but can be misleading because the person who commits the crime might not be dating the victim. Rather, it could be an acquaintance or stranger.
Codependency	Codependency is defined as a psychological condition or a relationship in which a person is controlled or manipulated by another who is affected with a pathological condition (typically narcissism or drug addiction); and in broader terms, it refers to the dependence on the needs of or control of another. It also often involves placing a lower priority on one's own needs, while being excessively preoccupied with the needs of others. Codependency can occur in any type of relationship, including family, work, friendship, and also romantic, peer or community relationships.
Enabling	Enabling is a term with a double meaning. As a positive term, it references patterns of interaction which allow individuals to develop and grow. These may be on any scale, for example within the family, or in wider society as 'Enabling acts' designed to empower some group, or create a new authority for a (usually governmental) body.
Adult Children of Alcoholics	Adult Children of Alcoholics is an organization that is intended to provide a forum to individuals who desire to recover from the effects of growing up in an alcoholic or otherwise dysfunctional family. ACA membership has few formal requirements.

Chapter 7. Alcohol: Behavioral Effects

Delirium tremens	Delirium tremens is an acute episode of delirium that is usually caused by withdrawal from alcohol, first described in 1813. Benzodiazepines are the treatment of choice for delirium tremens. Withdrawal from sedative-hypnotics other than alcohol, such as benzodiazepines, or barbiturates, can also result in seizures, delirium tremens, and death if not properly managed. Withdrawal from other drugs which are not sedative-hypnotics such as caffeine and cocaine do not have major medical complications, and are not life-threatening.
Disulfiram	Disulfiram is a drug discovered in the 1920s and used to support the treatment of chronic alcoholism by producing an acute sensitivity to alcohol. It blocks the processing of alcohol in the body by inhibiting acetaldehyde dehydrogenase thus causing an unpleasant reaction when alcohol is consumed. Disulfiram should be used in conjunction with counseling and support.
Naltrexone	Naltrexone is an opioid receptor antagonist used primarily in the management of alcohol dependence and opioid dependence. It is marketed in generic form as its hydrochloride salt, naltrexone hydrochloride, and marketed under the trade names Revia and Depade. In some countries including the United States, a once-monthly extended-release injectable formulation is marketed under the trade name Vivitrol.
Genogram	A genogram is a pictorial display of a person's family relationships and medical history. It goes beyond a traditional family tree by allowing the user to visualize hereditary patterns and psychological factors that punctuate relationships. It can be used to identify repetitive patterns of behavior and to recognize hereditary tendencies.
Psychodrama	Psychodrama is an action method, often used as a psychotherapy, in which clients use spontaneous dramatization, role playing and dramatic self-presentation to investigate and gain insight into their lives. Developed by Jacob L. Moreno, M.D. (1889-1974) psychodrama includes elements of theater, often conducted on a stage where props can be used. By closely recreating real-life situations, and acting them out in the present, clients have the opportunity to evaluate their behavior and more deeply understand a particular situation in their lives.

Chapter 7. Alcohol: Behavioral Effects

1. _____ is an international mutual aid movement founded in 1935 by Bill Wilson and Dr. Bob Smith (Bill W. and Dr. Bob) in Akron, Ohio. AA states that its 'primary purpose is to stay sober and help other alcoholics achieve sobriety'. With other early members, Wilson and Smith developed AA's Twelve Step program of spiritual and character development.

   a. Higher Power
   b. Alcoholics Anonymous
   c. Keeley Institute
   d. Tired and emotional

2. _____ is an action method, often used as a psychotherapy, in which clients use spontaneous dramatization, role playing and dramatic self-presentation to investigate and gain insight into their lives. Developed by Jacob L. Moreno, M.D. (1889-1974) _____ includes elements of theater, often conducted on a stage where props can be used. By closely recreating real-life situations, and acting them out in the present, clients have the opportunity to evaluate their behavior and more deeply understand a particular situation in their lives.

   a. Psychodrama
   b. Sociometry
   c. Ken Sprague
   d. Posse Comitatus Act

3. _____, as described in the DSM-IV, is a psychiatric diagnosis describing the recurring use of alcoholic beverages despite its negative consequences. _____ is sometimes referred to by the less specific term alcoholism. However, many definitions of alcoholism exist, and only some are compatible with _____.

   a. Alcohol abuse
   b. Alcohol dehydrogenase
   c. Alcohol dementia
   d. Alcohol dependence

4. _____ is an act of another party involving contact intended to cause feelings of physical pain, injury, or other physical suffering or bodily harm. _____ has been described among animals too, for example among the Adélie penguins. In most cases, children are the victims of _____, but adults can be the sufferers too.

   a. Physical abuse
   b. Women's shelter
   c. Riggins v. Nevada
   d. Calcium carbimide

5. . _____ is a broad term for problems with alcohol, and is generally used to mean compulsive and uncontrolled consumption of alcoholic beverages, usually to the detriment of the drinker's health, personal relationships, and social standing. It is medically considered a disease, specifically an addictive illness, and in psychiatry several other terms are used, specifically 'alcohol abuse' and 'alcohol dependence,' which have slightly different definitions.

In 1979 an expert World Health Organization committee discouraged the use of '_____' in medicine, preferring the category of 'alcohol dependence syndrome'.

a. Alcoholism
b. Immanuel Kant
c. Organized Crime Control Act
d. Alcohol dependence

1. b
2. a
3. a
4. a
5. a

You can take the complete Chapter Practice Test

for Chapter 7. Alcohol: Behavioral Effects
on all key terms, persons, places, and concepts.

Online 99 Cents

http://www.epub52.21.20957.7.cram101.com/

Use www.Cram101.com for all your study needs

including Cram101's online interactive problem solving labs in

chemistry, statistics, mathematics, and more.

Chapter 8. Narcotics (Opioids)

CHAPTER OUTLINE: KEY TERMS, PEOPLE, PLACES, CONCEPTS

Endorphin

Opium

Designer drug

Drug interaction

Narcotic

Codeine

Heroin

Tobacco

Crack cocaine

Oxycodone

Nervous system

Opioid

Side effect

Agonist

Naltrexone

Tramadol

Alcoholics Anonymous

Methadone

Morphine

Chapter 8. Narcotics (Opioids)
CHAPTER OUTLINE: KEY TERMS, PEOPLE, PLACES, CONCEPTS

_____ | Hydromorphone

_____ | Pethidine

_____ | Buprenorphine

_____ | Parkinson's disease

_____ | Dextromethorphan

CHAPTER HIGHLIGHTS & NOTES: KEY TERMS, PEOPLE, PLACES, CONCEPTS

| Endorphin | Endorphins ('endogenous morphine') are endogenous opioid peptides that function as neurotransmitters. They are produced by the pituitary gland and the hypothalamus in vertebrates during exercise, excitement, pain, consumption of spicy food, love and orgasm, and they resemble the opiates in their abilities to produce analgesia and a feeling of well-being.

The term 'endorphin' implies a pharmacological activity (analogous to the activity of the corticosteroid category of biochemicals) as opposed to a specific chemical formulation. |

| Opium | Opium is the dried latex obtained from the opium poppy (Papaver somniferum). Opium contains up to 12% morphine, an alkaloid, which is frequently processed chemically to produce heroin for the illegal drug trade. The latex also includes codeine and non-narcotic alkaloids such as papaverine, thebaine and noscapine. |

| Designer drug | Designer drug is a term used to describe drugs which are created (or marketed, if they had already existed) to get around existing drug laws, usually by modifying the molecular structures of existing drugs to varying degrees, or less commonly by finding drugs with entirely different chemical structures that produce similar subjective effects to illegal recreational drugs.

History

United States

1920s-1930s |

	The term 'designer drug' was first coined by law enforcement in the 1980s, and has gained widespread use. However the first appearance of what would now be termed designer drugs occurred well before this, in the 1920s.
Drug interaction	A drug interaction is a situation in which a substance affects the activity of a drug, i.e. the effects are increased or decreased, or they produce a new effect that neither produces on its own. Typically, interaction between drugs come to mind (drug-drug interaction). However, interactions may also exist between drugs & foods (drug-food interactions), as well as drugs & herbs (drug-herb interactions).
Narcotic	The term narcotic originally referred medically to any psychoactive compound with sleep-inducing properties. In the United States of America it has since become associated with opioids, commonly morphine and heroin. The term is, today, imprecisely defined and typically has negative connotations.
Codeine	Codeine is an opiate used for its analgesic, antitussive, and antidiarrheal properties. Codeine is the second-most predominant alkaloid in opium, at up to 3 percent; it is much more prevalent in the Iranian poppy (Papaver bractreatum), and codeine is extracted from this species in some places although the below-mentioned morphine methylation process is still much more common. It is considered the prototype of the weak to midrange opioids.
Heroin	Heroin (diacetylmorphine (INN)), also known as diamorphine (BAN), is a semi-synthetic opioid drug synthesized from morphine, a derivative of the opium poppy. It is the 3,6-diacetyl ester of morphine (di (two)-acetyl-morphine). The white crystalline form is commonly the hydrochloride salt diacetylmorphine hydrochloride, though often adulterated thus dulling the sheen and consistency from that to a matte white powder, which diacetylmorphine freebase typically is. 90% of diacetylmorphine is thought to be produced in Afghanistan.
Tobacco	Tobacco is an agricultural product processed from the leaves of plants in the genus Nicotiana. It can be consumed, used as an organic pesticide and, in the form of nicotine tartrate, used in some medicines. It is most commonly used as a recreational drug, and is a valuable cash crop for countries such as Cuba, China and the United States.
Crack cocaine	Crack cocaine is the freebase form of cocaine that can be smoked. It may also be termed rock, hard, iron, cavvy, base, or just crack.

Appearance and characteristics |

Chapter 8. Narcotics (Opioids)

Oxycodone	Oxycodone is an opioid analgesic medication synthesized from opium-derived thebaine. It was developed in 1916 in Germany, as one of several new semi-synthetic opioids in an attempt to improve on the existing opioids: morphine, diacetylmorphine (heroin), and codeine.
Nervous system	The nervous system is the part of an animal's body that coordinates the actions of the animal and transmits signals between different parts of its body. In most types of animals it consists of two main parts, the central nervous system and the peripheral nervous system. The CNS contains the brain and spinal cord.
Opioid	An opioid is a chemical that works by binding to opioid receptors, which are found principally in the central and peripheral nervous system and the gastrointestinal tract. The receptors in these organ systems mediate both the beneficial effects and the side effects of opioids. Opioids are among the world's oldest known drugs; the use of the opium poppy for its therapeutic benefits predates recorded history.
Side effect	In medicine, a side effect is an effect, whether therapeutic or adverse, that is secondary to the one intended; although the term is predominantly employed to describe adverse effects, it can also apply to beneficial, but unintended, consequences of the use of a drug. Occasionally, drugs are prescribed or procedures performed specifically for their side effects; in that case, said side effect ceases to be a side effect, and is now an intended effect. For instance, X-rays were historically (and are currently) used as an imaging technique; the discovery of their oncolytic capability led to their employ in radiotherapy (ablation of malignant tumours.
Agonist	An agonist is a chemical that binds to a receptor of a cell and triggers a response by that cell. Agonists often mimic the action of a naturally occurring substance. Whereas an agonist causes an action, an antagonist blocks the action of the agonist and an inverse agonist causes an action opposite to that of the agonist.
Naltrexone	Naltrexone is an opioid receptor antagonist used primarily in the management of alcohol dependence and opioid dependence. It is marketed in generic form as its hydrochloride salt, naltrexone hydrochloride, and marketed under the trade names Revia and Depade. In some countries including the United States, a once-monthly extended-release injectable formulation is marketed under the trade name Vivitrol.
Tramadol	Tramadol is a centrally acting opioid analgesic, used in treating moderate to severe pain. The drug has a wide range of applications, including treatment for restless leg syndrome and fibromyalgia. It was developed by the pharmaceutical company Grünenthal GmbH in the late 1970s.

Alcoholics Anonymous	Alcoholics Anonymous is an international mutual aid movement founded in 1935 by Bill Wilson and Dr. Bob Smith (Bill W. and Dr. Bob) in Akron, Ohio. AA states that its 'primary purpose is to stay sober and help other alcoholics achieve sobriety'. With other early members, Wilson and Smith developed AA's Twelve Step program of spiritual and character development.
Methadone	Methadone is a synthetic opioid, used medically as an analgesic and a maintenance anti-addictive for use in patients on opioids. It was developed in Germany in 1937. Although chemically unlike morphine or heroin, methadone also acts on the opioid receptors and thus produces many of the same effects. Methadone is also used in managing chronic pain owing to its long duration of action and very low cost.
Morphine	Supplementary data for morphine. Structure and properties
Hydromorphone	Hydromorphone is a very potent centrally-acting analgesic drug of the opioid class. It is a derivative of morphine, to be specific, a hydrogenated ketone thereof and, therefore, a semi-synthetic drug. It is, in medical terms, an opioid analgesic and, in legal terms, a narcotic.
Pethidine	Pethidine or meperidine (USAN) (commonly referred to as Demerol but also referred to as: isonipecaine; lidol; pethanol; piridosal; Algil; Alodan; Centralgin; Dispadol; Dolantin; Mialgin (in Indonesia); Petidin Dolargan (in Poland); Dolestine; Dolosal; Dolsin; Mefedina) is a fast-acting opioid analgesic drug. In the United States and Canada, it is more commonly known as meperidine or by its brand name Demerol. Pethidine was the first synthetic opioid synthesized in 1932 as a potential anti-spasmodic agent by the chemist Otto Eislib.
Buprenorphine	Buprenorphine is a semi-synthetic opioid that is used to treat opioid addiction in higher dosages (>2 mg), to control moderate acute pain in non-opioid-tolerant individuals in lower dosages (~200 µg), and to control moderate chronic pain in dosages ranging from 20-70 µg/hour. It is available in a variety of formulations: Subutex, Suboxone (typically used for opioid addiction), Temgesic, Buprenex (solutions for injection often used for acute pain in primary-care settings), Norspan and Butrans (transdermal preparations used for chronic pain). Buprenorphine hydrochloride was first marketed in the 1980s by Reckitt & Colman (now Reckitt Benckiser) as an analgesic, generally available as Temgesic 0.2 mg sublingual tablets, and as Buprenex in a 0.3 mg/ml injectable formulation.
Parkinson's disease	Parkinson's disease is a degenerative disorder of the central nervous system.

Chapter 8. Narcotics (Opioids)

	The motor symptoms of Parkinson's disease result from the death of dopamine-generating cells in the substantia nigra, a region of the midbrain; the cause of this cell death is unknown. Early in the course of the disease, the most obvious symptoms are movement-related; these include shaking, rigidity, slowness of movement and difficulty with walking and gait.
Dextromethorphan	Dextromethorphan is an antitussive (cough suppressant) drug. It is one of the active ingredients in many over-the-counter cold and cough medicines, such as Robitussin, NyQuil, Dimetapp, Vicks, Coricidin, Delsym, and others, including generic labels. Dextromethorphan has also found other uses in medicine, ranging from pain relief to psychological applications.

1. _____ is an opioid receptor antagonist used primarily in the management of alcohol dependence and opioid dependence. It is marketed in generic form as its hydrochloride salt, _____ hydrochloride, and marketed under the trade names Revia and Depade. In some countries including the United States, a once-monthly extended-release injectable formulation is marketed under the trade name Vivitrol.

   a. National Institute on Alcohol Abuse and Alcoholism
   b. The Natural History of Alcoholism Revisited
   c. Paddington alcohol test
   d. Naltrexone

2. An _____ is a chemical that works by binding to _____ receptors, which are found principally in the central and peripheral nervous system and the gastrointestinal tract. The receptors in these organ systems mediate both the beneficial effects and the side effects of _____s.

   _____s are among the world's oldest known drugs; the use of the opium poppy for its therapeutic benefits predates recorded history.

   a. Adrenorphin
   b. Akuammine
   c. Alvimopan
   d. Opioid

3. . _____ is a term used to describe drugs which are created (or marketed, if they had already existed) to get around existing drug laws, usually by modifying the molecular structures of existing drugs to varying degrees, or less commonly by finding drugs with entirely different chemical structures that produce similar subjective effects to illegal recreational drugs.

Chapter 8. Narcotics (Opioids)

History

United States

1920s-1930s

The term '_____' was first coined by law enforcement in the 1980s, and has gained widespread use. However the first appearance of what would now be termed _____s occurred well before this, in the 1920s.

a. Form constant
b. Designer drug
c. Hallucination
d. Hallucinogen persisting perception disorder

4. _____ is an agricultural product processed from the leaves of plants in the genus Nicotiana. It can be consumed, used as an organic pesticide and, in the form of nicotine tartrate, used in some medicines. It is most commonly used as a recreational drug, and is a valuable cash crop for countries such as Cuba, China and the United States.

a. Tobacco barn
b. Big Tobacco
c. British Doctors Study
d. Tobacco

5. _____ is the dried latex obtained from the _____ poppy (Papaver somniferum). _____ contains up to 12% morphine, an alkaloid, which is frequently processed chemically to produce heroin for the illegal drug trade. The latex also includes codeine and non-narcotic alkaloids such as papaverine, thebaine and noscapine.

a. Opium den
b. Opium lamp
c. Opium
d. Opium replacement

1. d
2. d
3. b
4. d
5. c

You can take the complete Chapter Practice Test

for Chapter 8. Narcotics (Opioids)
on all key terms, persons, places, and concepts.

Online 99 Cents

http://www.epub52.21.20957.8.cram101.com/

Use www.Cram101.com for all your study needs

including Cram101's online interactive problem solving labs in

chemistry, statistics, mathematics, and more.

Chapter 9. Stimulants

CHAPTER OUTLINE: KEY TERMS, PEOPLE, PLACES, CONCEPTS

Amphetamine

Designer drug

Drug interaction

Dopamine

Epinephrine

Hormone

Methylphenidate

Norepinephrine

Insomnia

Narcolepsy

Serotonin

Side effect

Sexual assault

Methamphetamine

Heroin

Domestic violence

Physical abuse

Stimulant

Alcoholics Anonymous

CHAPTER OUTLINE: KEY TERMS, PEOPLE, PLACES, CONCEPTS

_____ | Adderall _____

_____ | Modafinil _____

_____ | Cocaine _____

_____ | Neuron _____

_____ | Crack cocaine _____

_____ | Tobacco _____

_____ | Androstenedione _____

_____ | Caffeine _____

_____ | Cocaine dependence _____

_____ | Prevalence _____

_____ | Nervous system _____

_____ | Ephedrine _____

Chapter 9. Stimulants

Amphetamine	Amphetamine or amfetamine (INN) is a psychostimulant drug of the phenethylamine class that is known to produce increased wakefulness and focus in association with decreased fatigue and appetite. Brand names of medications that contain, or metabolize into, amphetamine include Adderall, Dexedrine, Dextrostat, Desoxyn, ProCentra, and Vyvanse, as well as Benzedrine in the past. The drug is also used recreationally and as a performance enhancer.
Designer drug	Designer drug is a term used to describe drugs which are created (or marketed, if they had already existed) to get around existing drug laws, usually by modifying the molecular structures of existing drugs to varying degrees, or less commonly by finding drugs with entirely different chemical structures that produce similar subjective effects to illegal recreational drugs. History United States 1920s-1930s The term 'designer drug' was first coined by law enforcement in the 1980s, and has gained widespread use. However the first appearance of what would now be termed designer drugs occurred well before this, in the 1920s.
Drug interaction	A drug interaction is a situation in which a substance affects the activity of a drug, i.e. the effects are increased or decreased, or they produce a new effect that neither produces on its own. Typically, interaction between drugs come to mind (drug-drug interaction). However, interactions may also exist between drugs & foods (drug-food interactions), as well as drugs & herbs (drug-herb interactions).
Dopamine	Dopamine a simple organic chemical in the catecholamine family, is a monoamine neurotransmitter, which has a number of important physiological roles in the bodies of animals. In addition to being a catecholamine and a monoamine, dopamine may be classified as a substituted phenethylamine. Its name derives from its chemical structure, which consists of an amine group (NH_2) linked to a catechol structure, called dihydroxyphenethylamine, the decarboxylated form of dihydroxyphenylalanine (acronym DOPA).
Epinephrine	Epinephrine is a hormone and a neurotransmitter. Epinephrine has many functions in the body, regulating heart rate, blood vessel and air passage diameters, and metabolic shifts; epinephrine release is a crucial component of the fight-or-flight response of the sympathetic nervous system.

Hormone	A hormone is a chemical released by a cell or a gland in one part of the body that sends out messages that affect cells in other parts of the organism. Only a little amount of hormone is required to alter cell metabolism. In essence, it is a chemical messenger that transports a signal from one cell to another.
Methylphenidate	Methylphenidate is a psychostimulant drug approved for treatment of attention-deficit hyperactivity disorder, postural orthostatic tachycardia syndrome, and narcolepsy. It may also be prescribed for off-label use in treatment-resistant cases of lethargy, depression, neural insult and obesity. Methylphenidate belongs to the piperidine class of compounds and increases the levels of dopamine and norepinephrine in the brain through reuptake inhibition of the monoamine transporters.
Norepinephrine	Norepinephrine is a catecholamine with multiple roles including as a hormone and a neurotransmitter. As a stress hormone, norepinephrine affects parts of the brain, such as the amygdala, where attention and responses are controlled. Along with epinephrine, norepinephrine also underlies the fight-or-flight response, directly increasing heart rate, triggering the release of glucose from energy stores, and increasing blood flow to skeletal muscle. It increases the brain's oxygen supply. Norepinephrine can also suppress neuroinflammation when released diffusely in the brain from the locus ceruleus.
Insomnia	Insomnia, is a sleep disorder in which there is an inability to fall asleep or to stay asleep as long as desired. While the term is sometimes used to describe a disorder demonstrated by polysomnographic evidence of disturbed sleep, insomnia is often practically defined as a positive response to either of two questions: 'Do you experience difficulty sleeping?' or 'Do you have difficulty falling or staying asleep?' Thus, insomnia is most often thought of as both a sign and a symptom that can accompany several sleep, medical, and psychiatric disorders characterized by a persistent difficulty falling asleep and/or staying asleep or sleep of poor quality. Insomnia is typically followed by functional impairment while awake.
Narcolepsy	Narcolepsy is a chronic neurological disorder caused by the brain's inability to regulate sleep-wake cycles normally. People with narcolepsy often experience disturbed nocturnal sleep and an abnormal daytime sleep pattern, which often is confused with insomnia. Narcoleptics, when falling asleep, generally experience the REM stage of sleep within 5 minutes, while most people do not experience REM sleep until an hour or so later.

Chapter 9. Stimulants

Serotonin	Serotonin is a monoamine neurotransmitter. Biochemically derived from tryptophan, serotonin is primarily found in the gastrointestinal (GI) tract, platelets, and in the central nervous system (CNS) of animals including humans. It is a well-known contributor to feelings of well-being; therefore it is also known as a 'happiness hormone' despite not being a hormone.
Side effect	In medicine, a side effect is an effect, whether therapeutic or adverse, that is secondary to the one intended; although the term is predominantly employed to describe adverse effects, it can also apply to beneficial, but unintended, consequences of the use of a drug.
	Occasionally, drugs are prescribed or procedures performed specifically for their side effects; in that case, said side effect ceases to be a side effect, and is now an intended effect. For instance, X-rays were historically (and are currently) used as an imaging technique; the discovery of their oncolytic capability led to their employ in radiotherapy (ablation of malignant tumours.
Sexual assault	Sexual assault is an assault of a sexual nature on another person, or any sexual act committed without consent. Although sexual assaults most frequently are by a man on a woman, it may involve any combination of two or more men, women and children.
	The term sexual assault is used, in public discourse, as a generic term that is defined as any involuntary sexual act in which a person is threatened, coerced, or forced to engage against their will, or any sexual touching of a person who has not consented.
Methamphetamine	Methamphetamine, methylamphetamine, N-methylamphetamine, desoxyephedrine, and colloquially as 'meth' or 'crystal meth', is a psychostimulant of the phenethylamine and amphetamine class of drugs. It increases alertness, concentration, energy, and in high doses, can induce euphoria, enhance self-esteem, and increase libido. Methamphetamine has high potential for abuse and addiction by activating the psychological reward system via triggering a cascading release of dopamine, norepinephrine and serotonin in the brain.
Heroin	Heroin (diacetylmorphine (INN)), also known as diamorphine (BAN), is a semi-synthetic opioid drug synthesized from morphine, a derivative of the opium poppy. It is the 3,6-diacetyl ester of morphine (di (two)-acetyl-morphine). The white crystalline form is commonly the hydrochloride salt diacetylmorphine hydrochloride, though often adulterated thus dulling the sheen and consistency from that to a matte white powder, which diacetylmorphine freebase typically is. 90% of diacetylmorphine is thought to be produced in Afghanistan.
Domestic violence	Domestic violence, spousal abuse, battering, family violence, and intimate partner violence (IPV), is defined as a pattern of abusive behaviors by one partner against another in an intimate relationship such as marriage, dating, family, or cohabitation.

Domestic violence, so defined, has many forms, including physical aggression or assault (hitting, kicking, biting, shoving, restraining, slapping, throwing objects), or threats thereof; sexual abuse; emotional abuse; controlling or domineering; intimidation; stalking; passive/covert abuse (e.g., neglect); and economic deprivation.

Alcohol consumption and mental illness can be co-morbid with abuse, and present additional challenges in eliminating domestic violence.

Physical abuse	Physical abuse is an act of another party involving contact intended to cause feelings of physical pain, injury, or other physical suffering or bodily harm. Physical abuse has been described among animals too, for example among the Adélie penguins. In most cases, children are the victims of physical abuse, but adults can be the sufferers too.
Stimulant	Stimulants (also called psychostimulants) are psychoactive drugs which induce temporary improvements in either mental or physical function or both. Examples of these kinds of effects may include enhanced alertness, wakefulness, and locomotion, among others. Due to their effects typically having an 'up' quality to them, stimulants are also occasionally referred to as 'uppers'.
Alcoholics Anonymous	Alcoholics Anonymous is an international mutual aid movement founded in 1935 by Bill Wilson and Dr. Bob Smith (Bill W. and Dr. Bob) in Akron, Ohio. AA states that its 'primary purpose is to stay sober and help other alcoholics achieve sobriety'. With other early members, Wilson and Smith developed AA's Twelve Step program of spiritual and character development.
Adderall	Adderall is a brand-name psychostimulant medication composed of racemic amphetamine aspartate monohydrate, racemic amphetamine sulfate, dextroamphetamine saccharide, and dextroamphetamine sulfate, which is thought by scientists to work by increasing the amount of dopamine and norepinephrine in the brain. In addition, the drug also acts as a potent dopamine reuptake inhibitor and norepinephrine reuptake inhibitor. Adderall is widely reported to increase alertness, increase libido, increase concentration and overall cognitive performance, and, in general, improve mood, while decreasing user fatigue.
Modafinil	Modafinil is an analeptic drug manufactured by Cephalon, and is approved by the U.S. Food and Drug Administration (FDA) for the treatment of narcolepsy, shift work sleep disorder, and excessive daytime sleepiness associated with obstructive sleep apnea. The European Medicines Agency has recommended that in Europe it be prescribed only for narcolepsy.
Cocaine	Cocaine benzoylmethylecgonine (INN) is a crystalline tropane alkaloid that is obtained from the leaves of the coca plant. The name comes from 'coca' in addition to the alkaloid suffix -ine, forming cocaine.

Chapter 9. Stimulants

Neuron	A neuron is an electrically excitable cell that processes and transmits information by electrical and chemical signaling. Chemical signaling occurs via synapses, specialized connections with other cells. Neurons connect to each other to form networks. Neurons are the core components of the nervous system, which includes the brain, spinal cord, and peripheral ganglia. A number of specialized types of neurons exist: sensory neurons respond to touch, sound, light and numerous other stimuli affecting cells of the sensory organs that then send signals to the spinal cord and brain. Motor neurons receive signals from the brain and spinal cord, cause muscle contractions, and affect glands. Interneurons connect neurons to other neurons within the same region of the brain or spinal cord.
Crack cocaine	Crack cocaine is the freebase form of cocaine that can be smoked. It may also be termed rock, hard, iron, cavvy, base, or just crack. Appearance and characteristics In purer forms, crack rocks appear as off-white nuggets with jagged edges, with a slightly higher density than candle wax.
Tobacco	Tobacco is an agricultural product processed from the leaves of plants in the genus Nicotiana. It can be consumed, used as an organic pesticide and, in the form of nicotine tartrate, used in some medicines. It is most commonly used as a recreational drug, and is a valuable cash crop for countries such as Cuba, China and the United States.
Androstenedione	Androstenedione is a 19-carbon steroid hormone produced in the adrenal glands and the gonads as an intermediate step in the biochemical pathway that produces the androgen testosterone and the estrogens estrone and estradiol.
Caffeine	Caffeine is a bitter, white crystalline xanthine alkaloid that acts as a stimulant drug. Caffeine is found in varying quantities in the seeds, leaves, and fruit of some plants, where it acts as a natural pesticide that paralyzes and kills certain insects feeding on the plants. It is most commonly consumed by humans in infusions extracted from the seed of the coffee plant and the leaves of the tea bush, as well as from various foods and drinks containing products derived from the kola nut.
Cocaine dependence	Cocaine dependence is psychological dependency on the regular use of cocaine. It can result in cardiovascular and brain damage, specifically in the central nervous system.

Chapter 9. Stimulants

Prevalence	In epidemiology, the prevalence of a health-related state (typically disease, but also other things like smoking or seatbelt use) in a statistical population is defined as the total number of cases of the risk factor in the population at a given time, or the total number of cases in the population, divided by the number of individuals in the population. It is used as an estimate of how common a disease is within a population over a certain period of time. It helps physicians or other health professionals understand the probability of certain diagnoses and is routinely used by epidemiologists, health care providers, government agencies and insurers.
Nervous system	The nervous system is the part of an animal's body that coordinates the actions of the animal and transmits signals between different parts of its body. In most types of animals it consists of two main parts, the central nervous system and the peripheral nervous system. The CNS contains the brain and spinal cord.
Ephedrine	Ephedrine is a sympathomimetic amine commonly used as a stimulant, appetite suppressant, concentration aid, decongestant, and to treat hypotension associated with anaesthesia. Ephedrine is similar in structure to the (semi-synthetic) derivatives amphetamine and methamphetamine. Chemically, it is an alkaloid derived from various plants in the genus Ephedra (family Ephedraceae).

CHAPTER QUIZ: KEY TERMS, PEOPLE, PLACES, CONCEPTS

1. _____ or amfetamine (INN) is a psychostimulant drug of the phenethylamine class that is known to produce increased wakefulness and focus in association with decreased fatigue and appetite.

Brand names of medications that contain, or metabolize into, _____ include Adderall, Dexedrine, Dextrostat, Desoxyn, ProCentra, and Vyvanse, as well as Benzedrine in the past.

The drug is also used recreationally and as a performance enhancer.

a. Aplindore
b. Apomorphine
c. Azapride
d. Amphetamine

2. . A _____ is an electrically excitable cell that processes and transmits information by electrical and chemical signaling. Chemical signaling occurs via synapses, specialized connections with other cells. _____s connect to each other to form networks.

Chapter 9. Stimulants

_____s are the core components of the nervous system, which includes the brain, spinal cord, and peripheral ganglia. A number of specialized types of _____s exist: sensory _____s respond to touch, sound, light and numerous other stimuli affecting cells of the sensory organs that then send signals to the spinal cord and brain. Motor _____s receive signals from the brain and spinal cord, cause muscle contractions, and affect glands.
Inter_____s connect _____s to other _____s within the same region of the brain or spinal cord.

a. Neuron
b. Convulsion
c. Posse Comitatus Act
d. D-IX

3. _____ is a catecholamine with multiple roles including as a hormone and a neurotransmitter.

As a stress hormone, _____ affects parts of the brain, such as the amygdala, where attention and responses are controlled. Along with epinephrine, _____ also underlies the fight-or-flight response, directly increasing heart rate, triggering the release of glucose from energy stores, and increasing blood flow to skeletal muscle. It increases the brain's oxygen supply. _____ can also suppress neuroinflammation when released diffusely in the brain from the locus ceruleus.

a. Catecholamine
b. substance P
c. Monoamine neurotransmitter
d. Norepinephrine

4. In medicine, a _____ is an effect, whether therapeutic or adverse, that is secondary to the one intended; although the term is predominantly employed to describe adverse effects, it can also apply to beneficial, but unintended, consequences of the use of a drug.

Occasionally, drugs are prescribed or procedures performed specifically for their _____s; in that case, said _____ ceases to be a _____, and is now an intended effect. For instance, X-rays were historically (and are currently) used as an imaging technique; the discovery of their oncolytic capability led to their employ in radiotherapy (ablation of malignant tumours.

a. safety monitoring
b. mechanism of action
c. Side effect
d. Therapeutic index

5. . _____ is an international mutual aid movement founded in 1935 by Bill Wilson and Dr. Bob Smith (Bill W. and Dr. Bob) in Akron, Ohio. AA states that its 'primary purpose is to stay sober and help other alcoholics achieve sobriety'. With other early members, Wilson and Smith developed AA's Twelve Step program of spiritual and character development.

a. Alcoholics Anonymous

b. History of Alcoholics Anonymous

c. Keeley Institute

d. Tired and emotional

1. d
2. a
3. d
4. c
5. a

You can take the complete Chapter Practice Test

for Chapter 9. Stimulants
on all key terms, persons, places, and concepts.

Online 99 Cents

http://www.epub52.21.20957.9.cram101.com/

Use www.Cram101.com for all your study needs

including Cram101's online interactive problem solving labs in

chemistry, statistics, mathematics, and more.

Chapter 10. Tobacco

CHAPTER OUTLINE: KEY TERMS, PEOPLE, PLACES, CONCEPTS

	Tobacco
	Drug interaction
	Cancer
	Cocaine
	Nervous system
	Neuron
	Chewing tobacco
	Electronic cigarette

CHAPTER HIGHLIGHTS & NOTES: KEY TERMS, PEOPLE, PLACES, CONCEPTS

Tobacco	Tobacco is an agricultural product processed from the leaves of plants in the genus Nicotiana. It can be consumed, used as an organic pesticide and, in the form of nicotine tartrate, used in some medicines. It is most commonly used as a recreational drug, and is a valuable cash crop for countries such as Cuba, China and the United States.
Drug interaction	A drug interaction is a situation in which a substance affects the activity of a drug, i.e. the effects are increased or decreased, or they produce a new effect that neither produces on its own. Typically, interaction between drugs come to mind (drug-drug interaction). However, interactions may also exist between drugs & foods (drug-food interactions), as well as drugs & herbs (drug-herb interactions).
Cancer	Cancer, known medically as a malignant neoplasm, is a broad group of various diseases, all involving unregulated cell growth. In cancer, cells divide and grow uncontrollably, forming malignant tumors, and invade nearby parts of the body. The cancer may also spread to more distant parts of the body through the lymphatic system or bloodstream.

Chapter 10. Tobacco

Cocaine	Cocaine benzoylmethylecgonine (INN) is a crystalline tropane alkaloid that is obtained from the leaves of the coca plant. The name comes from 'coca' in addition to the alkaloid suffix -ine, forming cocaine. It is a stimulant of the central nervous system, an appetite suppressant, and a topical anesthetic.
Nervous system	The nervous system is the part of an animal's body that coordinates the actions of the animal and transmits signals between different parts of its body. In most types of animals it consists of two main parts, the central nervous system and the peripheral nervous system. The CNS contains the brain and spinal cord.
Neuron	A neuron is an electrically excitable cell that processes and transmits information by electrical and chemical signaling. Chemical signaling occurs via synapses, specialized connections with other cells. Neurons connect to each other to form networks. Neurons are the core components of the nervous system, which includes the brain, spinal cord, and peripheral ganglia. A number of specialized types of neurons exist: sensory neurons respond to touch, sound, light and numerous other stimuli affecting cells of the sensory organs that then send signals to the spinal cord and brain. Motor neurons receive signals from the brain and spinal cord, cause muscle contractions, and affect glands. Interneurons connect neurons to other neurons within the same region of the brain or spinal cord.
Chewing tobacco	Chewing tobacco refers to a form of smokeless tobacco furnished as long strands of whole leaves and consumed by placing a portion of the tobacco between the cheek and gum or teeth and chewing. Unlike dipping tobacco, it is not ground and must be mechanically crushed with the teeth to release flavor and nicotine. Unwanted juices are then expectorated.
Electronic cigarette	An electronic cigarette, e-cigarette or vapor cigarette, is a battery-powered device that provides inhaled doses of nicotine or non-nicotine vaporized solution. It is an alternative to smoked tobacco products, such as a cigarette. In addition to nicotine delivery, the vapor also provides a flavor and physical sensation similar to that of inhaled tobacco smoke, although there is no tobacco, combustion or smoke present.

Chapter 10. Tobacco

CHAPTER QUIZ: KEY TERMS, PEOPLE, PLACES, CONCEPTS

1. A _____ is an electrically excitable cell that processes and transmits information by electrical and chemical signaling. Chemical signaling occurs via synapses, specialized connections with other cells. _____s connect to each other to form networks. _____s are the core components of the nervous system, which includes the brain, spinal cord, and peripheral ganglia. A number of specialized types of _____s exist: sensory _____s respond to touch, sound, light and numerous other stimuli affecting cells of the sensory organs that then send signals to the spinal cord and brain. Motor _____s receive signals from the brain and spinal cord, cause muscle contractions, and affect glands. Inter_____s connect _____s to other _____s within the same region of the brain or spinal cord.

   a. Past medical history
   b. Convulsion
   c. Neuron
   d. Neural decoding

2. The _____ is the part of an animal's body that coordinates the actions of the animal and transmits signals between different parts of its body. In most types of animals it consists of two main parts, the central _____ and the peripheral _____. The CNS contains the brain and spinal cord.

   a. Neural backpropagation
   b. Neural basis of self
   c. Nervous system
   d. Neural decoding

3. _____, known medically as a malignant neoplasm, is a broad group of various diseases, all involving unregulated cell growth. In _____, cells divide and grow uncontrollably, forming malignant tumors, and invade nearby parts of the body. The _____ may also spread to more distant parts of the body through the lymphatic system or bloodstream.

   a. Milkana G. Palavurova
   b. Cancer
   c. Morton Prince
   d. Biosimilar

4. _____ benzoylmethylecgonine (INN) is a crystalline tropane alkaloid that is obtained from the leaves of the coca plant. The name comes from 'coca' in addition to the alkaloid suffix -ine, forming _____. It is a stimulant of the central nervous system, an appetite suppressant, and a topical anesthetic.

   a. Cocaine paste
   b. Cocaine spoon
   c. Crack stem
   d. Cocaine

5. . _____ is an agricultural product processed from the leaves of plants in the genus Nicotiana. It can be consumed, used as an organic pesticide and, in the form of nicotine tartrate, used in some medicines. It is most commonly used as a recreational drug, and is a valuable cash crop for countries such as Cuba, China and the United States.

Visit Cram101.com for full Practice Exams

Chapter 10. Tobacco

a. Tobacco barn
b. Big Tobacco
c. Tobacco
d. Burley

ANSWER KEY
Chapter 10. Tobacco

1. c
2. c
3. b
4. d
5. c

You can take the complete Chapter Practice Test

for Chapter 10. Tobacco
on all key terms, persons, places, and concepts.

Online 99 Cents

http://www.epub52.21.20957.10.cram101.com/

Use www.Cram101.com for all your study needs

including Cram101's online interactive problem solving labs in

chemistry, statistics, mathematics, and more.

Chapter 11. Hallucinogens (Psychedelics)

CHAPTER OUTLINE: KEY TERMS, PEOPLE, PLACES, CONCEPTS

- Mescaline
- Psychotomimetic
- Synesthesia
- Flashback
- Side effect
- Psilocybin
- Amphetamine
- Designer drug
- Drug interaction
- Ecstasy
- Atropa belladonna
- Datura stramonium
- Catatonia
- Ketamine
- Dextromethorphan
- Hallucination
- Nervous system
- Salvia divinorum

Chapter 11. Hallucinogens (Psychedelics)

Mescaline	Mescaline is a naturally-occurring psychedelic alkaloid of the phenethylamine class used mainly as an entheogen. It occurs naturally in the peyote cactus (Lophophora williamsii), the San Pedro cactus (Echinopsis pachanoi) and the Peruvian Torch cactus (Echinopsis peruviana), and in a number of other members of the Cactaceae plant family. It is also found in small amounts in certain members of the Fabaceae (bean) family, including Acacia berlandieri.
Psychotomimetic	A drug with psychotomimetic actions mimics the symptoms of psychosis, including delusions and/or delirium, as opposed to just hallucinations. Some drugs of the opioid class have psychotomimetic effects, such as pentazocine and butorphanolX' to describe the effects of cannabis.
Synesthesia	Synesthesia, from the ancient Greek σ?v (syn), 'together,' and α?σθησις (aisthesis), 'sensation,'is a neurologically-based condition in which stimulation of one sensory or cognitive pathway leads to automatic, involuntary experiences in a second sensory or cognitive pathway. People who report such experiences are known as synesthetes. In one common form of synesthesia, known as grapheme → color synesthesia or color-graphemic synesthesia, letters or numbers are perceived as inherently colored, while in ordinal linguistic personification, numbers, days of the week and months of the year evoke personalities.
Flashback	A flashback, is a psychological phenomenon in which an individual has a sudden, usually powerful, re-experiencing of a past experience or elements of a past experience. These experiences can be happy, sad, exciting, or any other emotion one can consider. The term is used particularly when the memory is recalled involuntarily, and/or when it is so intense that the person 'relives' the experience, unable to fully recognize it as memory and not something that is happening in 'real time'.
Side effect	In medicine, a side effect is an effect, whether therapeutic or adverse, that is secondary to the one intended; although the term is predominantly employed to describe adverse effects, it can also apply to beneficial, but unintended, consequences of the use of a drug. Occasionally, drugs are prescribed or procedures performed specifically for their side effects; in that case, said side effect ceases to be a side effect, and is now an intended effect. For instance, X-rays were historically (and are currently) used as an imaging technique; the discovery of their oncolytic capability led to their employ in radiotherapy (ablation of malignant tumours.

Chapter 11. Hallucinogens (Psychedelics)

CHAPTER HIGHLIGHTS & NOTES: KEY TERMS, PEOPLE, PLACES, CONCEPTS

Psilocybin	Psilocybin is a prodrug for the classical hallucinogen compound psilocin, or 4-HO-DMT (4-hydroxyl-dimethyltryptamine), the active metabolite of psilocybin, responsible the psychoactive effects of the drug. Both drugs are members of the indole and tryptamine classes. Psilocybin-containing mushrooms are used both recreationally, and traditionally, for spiritual purposes, as entheogens, with a history of use spanning millennia.
Amphetamine	Amphetamine or amfetamine (INN) is a psychostimulant drug of the phenethylamine class that is known to produce increased wakefulness and focus in association with decreased fatigue and appetite.
	Brand names of medications that contain, or metabolize into, amphetamine include Adderall, Dexedrine, Dextrostat, Desoxyn, ProCentra, and Vyvanse, as well as Benzedrine in the past.
	The drug is also used recreationally and as a performance enhancer.
Designer drug	Designer drug is a term used to describe drugs which are created (or marketed, if they had already existed) to get around existing drug laws, usually by modifying the molecular structures of existing drugs to varying degrees, or less commonly by finding drugs with entirely different chemical structures that produce similar subjective effects to illegal recreational drugs.
	History
	United States
	1920s-1930s
	The term 'designer drug' was first coined by law enforcement in the 1980s, and has gained widespread use. However the first appearance of what would now be termed designer drugs occurred well before this, in the 1920s.
Drug interaction	A drug interaction is a situation in which a substance affects the activity of a drug, i.e. the effects are increased or decreased, or they produce a new effect that neither produces on its own. Typically, interaction between drugs come to mind (drug-drug interaction). However, interactions may also exist between drugs & foods (drug-food interactions), as well as drugs & herbs (drug-herb interactions).
Ecstasy	Ecstasy (or ekstasis) from the Ancient Greek, ?κ-στασις (ek-stasis), is a subjective experience of total involvement of the subject, with an object of his or her awareness.

Because total involvement with an object of our interest is not our ordinary experience since we are ordinarily aware also of other objects, the ecstasy is an example of altered state of consciousness characterized by diminished awareness of other objects or total lack of the awareness of surroundings and everything around the object. For instance, if one is concentrating on a physical task, then one might cease to be aware of any intellectual thoughts.

Atropa belladonna	Atropa belladonna is a perennial herbaceous plant in the family Solanaceae, native to Europe, North Africa, and Western Asia. The foliage and berries are extremely toxic, containing tropane alkaloids. These toxins include scopolamine and hyoscyamine which cause a bizarre delirium and hallucinations, and are also used as pharmaceutical anticholinergics. The drug atropine is derived from the plant.
Datura stramonium	Datura stramonium It is an erect annual herb forming a bush up to 3-5 ft (1-1.5 m) tall. The leaves are soft, irregularly undulate, and toothed. The fragrant flowers are trumpet-shaped, white to creamy or violet, and 2.5 to 3.5 in. long. They rarely open completely. The egg-shaped seed capsule is walnut-sized and either covered with spines or bald. At maturity it splits into four chambers, each with dozens of small black seeds.Parts of the plant, especially the seeds and leaves, are sometimes used as a hallucinogen. Due to the elevated risk of overdose in uninformed users, many hospitalizations, and some deaths, are reported from this use.
Catatonia	Catatonia is a state of neurogenic motor immobility, and behavioral abnormality manifested by stupor. It was first described, in 1874, by Karl Ludwig Kahlbaum in Die Katatonie oder das Spannungsirresein (Catatonia or Tension Insanity). In the current Diagnostic and Statistical Manual of Mental Disorders published by the American Psychiatric Association (DSM-IV-TR) it is not recognized as a separate disorder, but is associated with psychiatric conditions such as schizophrenia (catatonic type), bipolar disorder, post-traumatic stress disorder, depression and other mental disorders, as well as drug abuse or overdose .
Ketamine	Ketamine is a drug used in human and veterinary medicine. Its hydrochloride salt is sold as Ketanest, Ketaset, and Ketalar. Pharmacologically, ketamine is classified as an NMDA receptor antagonist.
Dextromethorphan	Dextromethorphan is an antitussive (cough suppressant) drug. It is one of the active ingredients in many over-the-counter cold and cough medicines, such as Robitussin, NyQuil, Dimetapp, Vicks, Coricidin, Delsym, and others, including generic labels. Dextromethorphan has also found other uses in medicine, ranging from pain relief to psychological applications.
Hallucination	A hallucination, in the broadest sense of the word, is a perception in the absence of a stimulus.

In a stricter sense, hallucinations are defined as perceptions in a conscious and awake state in the absence of external stimuli which have qualities of real perception, in that they are vivid, substantial, and located in external objective space. The latter definition distinguishes hallucinations from the related phenomena of dreaming, which does not involve wakefulness; illusion, which involves distorted or misinterpreted real perception; imagery, which does not mimic real perception and is under voluntary control; and pseudohallucination, which does not mimic real perception, but is not under voluntary control.

Nervous system	The nervous system is the part of an animal's body that coordinates the actions of the animal and transmits signals between different parts of its body. In most types of animals it consists of two main parts, the central nervous system and the peripheral nervous system. The CNS contains the brain and spinal cord.
Salvia divinorum	Salvia divinorum is a psychoactive plant which can induce dissociative effects and is a potent producer of 'visions' and other hallucinatory experiences. Its native habitat is within cloud forest in the isolated Sierra Mazateca of Oaxaca, Mexico, where it grows in shady and moist locations. The plant grows to over a meter high, has hollow square stems, large leaves, and occasional white flowers with violet calyxes.

CHAPTER QUIZ: KEY TERMS, PEOPLE, PLACES, CONCEPTS

1. _____ is an antitussive (cough suppressant) drug. It is one of the active ingredients in many over-the-counter cold and cough medicines, such as Robitussin, NyQuil, Dimetapp, Vicks, Coricidin, Delsym, and others, including generic labels. _____ has also found other uses in medicine, ranging from pain relief to psychological applications.

   a. Dextromethorphan
   b. Fluvoxamine
   c. Lubazodone
   d. Panuramine

2. . _____ (or ekstasis) from the Ancient Greek, ?κ-στασις (ek-stasis), is a subjective experience of total involvement of the subject, with an object of his or her awareness. Because total involvement with an object of our interest is not our ordinary experience since we are ordinarily aware also of other objects, the _____ is an example of altered state of consciousness characterized by diminished awareness of other objects or total lack of the awareness of surroundings and everything around the object. For instance, if one is concentrating on a physical task, then one might cease to be aware of any intellectual thoughts.

   a. Embarrassment
   b. Epiphany

c. Insignificance

d. Ecstasy

3. _____ or amfetamine (INN) is a psychostimulant drug of the phenethylamine class that is known to produce increased wakefulness and focus in association with decreased fatigue and appetite.

Brand names of medications that contain, or metabolize into, _____ include Adderall, Dexedrine, Dextrostat, Desoxyn, ProCentra, and Vyvanse, as well as Benzedrine in the past.

The drug is also used recreationally and as a performance enhancer.

a. Aplindore

b. Apomorphine

c. Azapride

d. Amphetamine

4. In medicine, a _____ is an effect, whether therapeutic or adverse, that is secondary to the one intended; although the term is predominantly employed to describe adverse effects, it can also apply to beneficial, but unintended, consequences of the use of a drug.

Occasionally, drugs are prescribed or procedures performed specifically for their _____s; in that case, said _____ ceases to be a _____, and is now an intended effect. For instance, X-rays were historically (and are currently) used as an imaging technique; the discovery of their oncolytic capability led to their employ in radiotherapy (ablation of malignant tumours).

a. safety monitoring

b. Side effect

c. Benzoylecgonine

d. Therapeutic index

5. _____ is a naturally-occurring psychedelic alkaloid of the phenethylamine class used mainly as an entheogen.

It occurs naturally in the peyote cactus (Lophophora williamsii), the San Pedro cactus (Echinopsis pachanoi) and the Peruvian Torch cactus (Echinopsis peruviana), and in a number of other members of the Cactaceae plant family. It is also found in small amounts in certain members of the Fabaceae (bean) family, including Acacia berlandieri.

a. Quinine

b. Mescaline

c. Riggins v. Nevada

d. Metrosexual

1. a
2. d
3. d
4. b
5. b

Chapter 12. Marijuana

CHAPTER OUTLINE: KEY TERMS, PEOPLE, PLACES, CONCEPTS

- Cannabis
- Monitoring
- Peer group
- Nervous system
- Side effect
- Critical thinking
- Motivation
- Amotivational syndrome
- Heroin
- Antidepressant
- Glaucoma
- Muscle relaxant
- Fertility
- Alprazolam
- Anandamide
- Cocaine
- Aphrodisiac
- Psychological dependence

Chapter 12. Marijuana

Cannabis	Cannabis is a genus of flowering plants that includes three putative varieties, Cannabis sativa, Cannabis indica, and Cannabis ruderalis. These three taxa are indigenous to Central Asia, and South Asia. Cannabis has long been used for fibre (hemp), for seed and seed oils, for medicinal purposes, and as a recreational drug.
Monitoring	In medicine, monitoring is the observation of a disease, condition or one or several medical parameters over time. It can be performed by continuously measuring certain parameters by using a medical monitor (for example, by continuously measuring vital signs by a bedside monitor), and/or by repeatedly performing medical tests (such as blood glucose monitoring with a glucose meter in people with diabetes mellitus). Transmitting data from a monitor to a distant monitoring station is known as telemetry or biotelemetry.
Peer group	A peer group is a social group consisting of people. Peer groups are an informal primary group of people who share a similar or equal status and who are usually of roughly the same age, tended to travel around and interact within the social aggregate Members of a particular peer group often have similar interests and backgrounds, bonded by the premise of sameness. However, some peer groups are very diverse, crossing social divides such as socioeconomic status, level of education, race, creed, culture, or religion.
Nervous system	The nervous system is the part of an animal's body that coordinates the actions of the animal and transmits signals between different parts of its body. In most types of animals it consists of two main parts, the central nervous system and the peripheral nervous system. The CNS contains the brain and spinal cord.
Side effect	In medicine, a side effect is an effect, whether therapeutic or adverse, that is secondary to the one intended; although the term is predominantly employed to describe adverse effects, it can also apply to beneficial, but unintended, consequences of the use of a drug. Occasionally, drugs are prescribed or procedures performed specifically for their side effects; in that case, said side effect ceases to be a side effect, and is now an intended effect. For instance, X-rays were historically (and are currently) used as an imaging technique; the discovery of their oncolytic capability led to their employ in radiotherapy (ablation of malignant tumours.
Critical thinking	Critical thinking is a type of reasonable, reflective thinking that is aimed at deciding what to believe or what to do. It is a way of deciding whether a claim is always true, sometimes true, partly true, or false.

Chapter 12. Marijuana

Motivation	Motivation is the psychological feature that arouses an organism to action toward a desired goal and elicits, controls, and sustains certain goal directed behaviors. It can be considered a driving force; a psychological drive that compels or reinforces an action toward a desired goal. Motivation elicits, controls, and sustains certain goal-directed behaviors.
Amotivational syndrome	Amotivational syndrome is a psychological condition associated with diminished inspiration to participate in social situations and activities, with lapses in apathy caused by an external event, situation, substance, relationship, or other cause. While some have claimed that chronic use of cannabis causes amotivational syndrome in some users, empirical studies suggest that there is no such thing as 'amotivational syndrome', per se. From a World Health Organization report: A study done by researchers Barnwell, Earleywine and Wilcox on a sample of undergraduates also suggests that cannabis use does not cause an amotivational syndrome.
Heroin	Heroin (diacetylmorphine (INN)), also known as diamorphine (BAN), is a semi-synthetic opioid drug synthesized from morphine, a derivative of the opium poppy. It is the 3,6-diacetyl ester of morphine (di (two)-acetyl-morphine). The white crystalline form is commonly the hydrochloride salt diacetylmorphine hydrochloride, though often adulterated thus dulling the sheen and consistency from that to a matte white powder, which diacetylmorphine freebase typically is. 90% of diacetylmorphine is thought to be produced in Afghanistan.
Antidepressant	Antidepressants, despite their name, are often used to treat other conditions, on- or off-label, for conditions such as anxiety disorders, obsessive compulsive disorder, eating disorders, chronic pain, and some hormone-mediated disorders such as dysmenorrhea, and for snoring, migraines, attention-deficit hyperactivity disorder, (ADHD) substance abuse and occasionally even insomnia. Antidepressants are used either alone or combination with other medications. Most antidepressants have a delayed onset of action (2-6 weeks) but for responders, efficacy is often seen after one week.
Glaucoma	Glaucoma is an eye disorder in which the optic nerve suffers damage, permanently impacting vision in the affected eye(s) and progressing to complete blindness if untreated. It is often, but not always, associated with increased pressure of the fluid in the eye (aqueous humour). The nerve damage involves loss of retinal ganglion cells in a characteristic pattern.
Muscle relaxant	A muscle relaxant is a drug which affects skeletal muscle function and decreases the muscle tone. It may be used to alleviate symptoms such as muscle spasms, pain, and hyperreflexia.

Fertility	Fertility is the natural capability of giving life. As a measure, 'fertility rate' is the number of children born per couple, person or population. Fertility differs from fecundity, which is defined as the potential for reproduction (influenced by gamete production, fertilisation and carrying a pregnancy to term). Infertility is a deficient fertility.
Alprazolam	Alprazolam is a potent short-acting drug of the benzodiazepine class. It is primarily used to treat moderate to severe anxiety disorders (e.g., social anxiety disorder) and panic attacks, and is used as an adjunctive treatment for anxiety associated with moderate depression. It is available in an instant release and an extended-release (Xanax XR) preparation, both of which are available under several generic names.
Anandamide	Anandamide, is an endogenous cannabinoid neurotransmitter. It was isolated and its structure was first described by Czech analytical chemist Lumír Ondrej Hanuš and American molecular pharmacologist William Anthony Devane in 1992. The name is taken from the Sanskrit word ananda, which means 'bliss, delight', and amide. It is synthesized from N-arachidonoyl phosphatidylethanolamine by multiple pathways. It is degraded primarily by the fatty acid amide hydrolase (FAAH) enzyme, which converts anandamide into ethanolamine and arachidonic acid. As such, inhibitors of FAAH lead to elevated anandamide levels and are being pursued for therapeutic use.
Cocaine	Cocaine benzoylmethylecgonine (INN) is a crystalline tropane alkaloid that is obtained from the leaves of the coca plant. The name comes from 'coca' in addition to the alkaloid suffix -ine, forming cocaine. It is a stimulant of the central nervous system, an appetite suppressant, and a topical anesthetic.
Aphrodisiac	An aphrodisiac is a substance that increases sexual desire. The name comes from Aphrodite, the Greek goddess of sexuality and love. Throughout history, many foods, drinks, and behaviors have had a reputation for making sex more attainable and/or pleasurable.
Psychological dependence	In the APA Dictionary of Psychology, psychological dependence is defined as 'dependence on a psychoactive substance for the reinforcement it provides.' Most times psychological dependence is classified under addiction. They are similar in that addiction is a physiological 'craving' for something and psychological dependence is a 'need' for a particular substance because it causes enjoyable mental affects.

A person becomes dependent on something to help alleviate specific emotions. |

Chapter 12. Marijuana

1. In the APA Dictionary of Psychology, _____ is defined as 'dependence on a psychoactive substance for the reinforcement it provides.' Most times _____ is classified under addiction. They are similar in that addiction is a physiological 'craving' for something and _____ is a 'need' for a particular substance because it causes enjoyable mental affects.

   A person becomes dependent on something to help alleviate specific emotions.

   a. Psychological dependence
   b. Self-medication
   c. Slip
   d. Sober companion

2. The _____ is the part of an animal's body that coordinates the actions of the animal and transmits signals between different parts of its body. In most types of animals it consists of two main parts, the central _____ and the peripheral _____. The CNS contains the brain and spinal cord.

   a. Neural backpropagation
   b. Neural basis of self
   c. Neural coding
   d. Nervous system

3. _____ is a genus of flowering plants that includes three putative varieties, _____ sativa, _____ indica, and _____ ruderalis. These three taxa are indigenous to Central Asia, and South Asia. _____ has long been used for fibre (hemp), for seed and seed oils, for medicinal purposes, and as a recreational drug.

   a. Hard and soft drugs
   b. Journal of Psychoactive Drugs
   c. Cannabis
   d. Spins

4. A _____ is a social group consisting of people. _____s are an informal primary group of people who share a similar or equal status and who are usually of roughly the same age, tended to travel around and interact within the social aggregate Members of a particular _____ often have similar interests and backgrounds, bonded by the premise of sameness. However, some _____s are very diverse, crossing social divides such as socioeconomic status, level of education, race, creed, culture, or religion.

   a. Household
   b. Posse Comitatus Act
   c. Peer group
   d. Nerve guidance conduit

5. . In medicine, _____ is the observation of a disease, condition or one or several medical parameters over time.

It can be performed by continuously measuring certain parameters by using a medical monitor (for example, by continuously measuring vital signs by a bedside monitor), and/or by repeatedly performing medical tests (such as blood glucose _____ with a glucose meter in people with diabetes mellitus).

Transmitting data from a monitor to a distant _____ station is known as telemetry or biotelemetry.

a. Motor imagery
b. Motor unit number estimation
c. Monitoring
d. Nerve guidance conduit

ANSWER KEY
Chapter 12. Marijuana

1. a
2. d
3. c
4. c
5. c

You can take the complete Chapter Practice Test

for Chapter 12. Marijuana
on all key terms, persons, places, and concepts.

Online 99 Cents

http://www.epub52.21.20957.12.cram101.com/

Use www.Cram101.com for all your study needs

including Cram101's online interactive problem solving labs in

chemistry, statistics, mathematics, and more.

Chapter 13. Inhalants

CHAPTER OUTLINE: KEY TERMS, PEOPLE, PLACES, CONCEPTS

	Cardiac dysrhythmia
	Cocaine
	Side effect
	Poppers
	Nervous system
	Alcoholics Anonymous

CHAPTER HIGHLIGHTS & NOTES: KEY TERMS, PEOPLE, PLACES, CONCEPTS

Cardiac dysrhythmia	Cardiac dysrhythmia is a term for any of a large and heterogeneous group of conditions in which there is abnormal electrical activity in the heart. The heart beat may be too fast or too slow, and may be regular or irregular.

Some arrhythmias are life-threatening medical emergencies that can result in cardiac arrest and sudden death. Others cause symptoms such as an abnormal awareness of heart beat (palpitations), and may be merely annoying. These palpitations have also been known to be caused by atrial/ventricular fibrillation, wire faults, and other technical or mechanical issues in cardiac pacemakers/defibrillators. Still others may not be associated with any symptoms at all, but may predispose the patient to potentially life threatening stroke or embolism. |
| Cocaine | Cocaine benzoylmethylecgonine (INN) is a crystalline tropane alkaloid that is obtained from the leaves of the coca plant. The name comes from 'coca' in addition to the alkaloid suffix -ine, forming cocaine. It is a stimulant of the central nervous system, an appetite suppressant, and a topical anesthetic. |
| Side effect | In medicine, a side effect is an effect, whether therapeutic or adverse, that is secondary to the one intended; although the term is predominantly employed to describe adverse effects, it can also apply to beneficial, but unintended, consequences of the use of a drug. |

Chapter 13. Inhalants

Occasionally, drugs are prescribed or procedures performed specifically for their side effects; in that case, said side effect ceases to be a side effect, and is now an intended effect. For instance, X-rays were historically (and are currently) used as an imaging technique; the discovery of their oncolytic capability led to their employ in radiotherapy (ablation of malignant tumours).

Poppers

Poppers is a slang term for various alkyl nitrites inhaled for recreational purposes, particularly isopropyl nitrite (2-propyl nitrite) and isobutyl nitrite (2-methylpropyl nitrite), and now more rarely, butyl nitrite and amyl nitrite (isoamyl nitrite, isopentyl nitrite). Amyl nitrite is used medically as an antidote to cyanide poisoning, but the term 'poppers' refers specifically to recreational use. Amyl nitrite and several other alkyl nitrites, which are present in products such as air freshener, video head cleaner and finger nail polish remover, are often inhaled with the goal of enhancing sexual pleasure.

Nervous system

The nervous system is the part of an animal's body that coordinates the actions of the animal and transmits signals between different parts of its body. In most types of animals it consists of two main parts, the central nervous system and the peripheral nervous system. The CNS contains the brain and spinal cord.

Alcoholics Anonymous

Alcoholics Anonymous is an international mutual aid movement founded in 1935 by Bill Wilson and Dr. Bob Smith (Bill W. and Dr. Bob) in Akron, Ohio. AA states that its 'primary purpose is to stay sober and help other alcoholics achieve sobriety'. With other early members, Wilson and Smith developed AA's Twelve Step program of spiritual and character development.

1. . _____ is a term for any of a large and heterogeneous group of conditions in which there is abnormal electrical activity in the heart. The heart beat may be too fast or too slow, and may be regular or irregular.

Some arrhythmias are life-threatening medical emergencies that can result in cardiac arrest and sudden death. Others cause symptoms such as an abnormal awareness of heart beat (palpitations), and may be merely annoying. These palpitations have also been known to be caused by atrial/ventricular fibrillation, wire faults, and other technical or mechanical issues in cardiac pacemakers/defibrillators. Still others may not be associated with any symptoms at all, but may predispose the patient to potentially life threatening stroke or embolism.

a. Myocardial infarction
b. Posse Comitatus Act
c. Cardiac dysrhythmia

Chapter 13. Inhalants

2. _____ is a slang term for various alkyl nitrites inhaled for recreational purposes, particularly isopropyl nitrite (2-propyl nitrite) and isobutyl nitrite (2-methylpropyl nitrite), and now more rarely, butyl nitrite and amyl nitrite (isoamyl nitrite, isopentyl nitrite). Amyl nitrite is used medically as an antidote to cyanide poisoning, but the term '_____' refers specifically to recreational use. Amyl nitrite and several other alkyl nitrites, which are present in products such as air freshener, video head cleaner and finger nail polish remover, are often inhaled with the goal of enhancing sexual pleasure.

   a. Solenostemon scutellarioides
   b. Spins
   c. Cannabis
   d. Poppers

3. _____ benzoylmethylecgonine (INN) is a crystalline tropane alkaloid that is obtained from the leaves of the coca plant. The name comes from 'coca' in addition to the alkaloid suffix -ine, forming _____. It is a stimulant of the central nervous system, an appetite suppressant, and a topical anesthetic.

   a. Cocaine paste
   b. Cocaine spoon
   c. Cocaine
   d. D-IX

4. In medicine, a _____ is an effect, whether therapeutic or adverse, that is secondary to the one intended; although the term is predominantly employed to describe adverse effects, it can also apply to beneficial, but unintended, consequences of the use of a drug.

   Occasionally, drugs are prescribed or procedures performed specifically for their _____s; in that case, said _____ ceases to be a _____, and is now an intended effect. For instance, X-rays were historically (and are currently) used as an imaging technique; the discovery of their oncolytic capability led to their employ in radiotherapy (ablation of malignant tumours.

   a. safety monitoring
   b. Side effect
   c. Benzoylecgonine
   d. Therapeutic index

5. _____ is an international mutual aid movement founded in 1935 by Bill Wilson and Dr. Bob Smith (Bill W. and Dr. Bob) in Akron, Ohio. AA states that its 'primary purpose is to stay sober and help other alcoholics achieve sobriety'. With other early members, Wilson and Smith developed AA's Twelve Step program of spiritual and character development.

   a. Higher Power
   b. Alcoholics Anonymous
   c. Keeley Institute
   d. Tired and emotional

Visit Cram101.com for full Practice Exams

1. c
2. d
3. c
4. b
5. b

You can take the complete Chapter Practice Test

for Chapter 13. Inhalants
on all key terms, persons, places, and concepts.

Online 99 Cents

http://www.epub52.21.20957.13.cram101.com/

Use www.Cram101.com for all your study needs

including Cram101's online interactive problem solving labs in

chemistry, statistics, mathematics, and more.

Chapter 14. Over-the-Counter, Prescription, and Herbal Drugs

CHAPTER OUTLINE: KEY TERMS, PEOPLE, PLACES, CONCEPTS

- Ephedrine
- Designer drug
- Reye's syndrome
- Caffeine
- Nervous system
- Side effect
- Pseudoephedrine
- Methamphetamine
- Diphenhydramine
- Insomnia
- Amphetamine
- Depressant
- Dextromethorphan
- Stimulant
- Drug interaction
- Toxicity
- Antidepressant
- Depression
- Bronchodilator

	Edema
	Hypertension
	Cocaine
	Adderall
	Hypothyroidism
	Methylphenidate
	Anabolic steroid
	Crack cocaine

CHAPTER HIGHLIGHTS & NOTES: KEY TERMS, PEOPLE, PLACES, CONCEPTS

| Ephedrine | Ephedrine is a sympathomimetic amine commonly used as a stimulant, appetite suppressant, concentration aid, decongestant, and to treat hypotension associated with anaesthesia.

Ephedrine is similar in structure to the (semi-synthetic) derivatives amphetamine and methamphetamine. Chemically, it is an alkaloid derived from various plants in the genus Ephedra (family Ephedraceae). |
|---|---|
| Designer drug | Designer drug is a term used to describe drugs which are created (or marketed, if they had already existed) to get around existing drug laws, usually by modifying the molecular structures of existing drugs to varying degrees, or less commonly by finding drugs with entirely different chemical structures that produce similar subjective effects to illegal recreational drugs.

History

United States

1920s-1930s |

Chapter 14. Over-the-Counter, Prescription, and Herbal Drugs

	The term 'designer drug' was first coined by law enforcement in the 1980s, and has gained widespread use. However the first appearance of what would now be termed designer drugs occurred well before this, in the 1920s.
Reye's syndrome	Reye's syndrome is a potentially fatal disease that causes numerous detrimental effects to many organs, especially the brain and liver, as well as causing a lower than usual level of blood sugar (hypoglycemia). The classic features are liver damage, aspirin use and a viral infection. The exact cause is unknown, and while it has been associated with aspirin consumption by children with viral illness, it also occurs in the absence of aspirin use.
Caffeine	Caffeine is a bitter, white crystalline xanthine alkaloid that acts as a stimulant drug. Caffeine is found in varying quantities in the seeds, leaves, and fruit of some plants, where it acts as a natural pesticide that paralyzes and kills certain insects feeding on the plants. It is most commonly consumed by humans in infusions extracted from the seed of the coffee plant and the leaves of the tea bush, as well as from various foods and drinks containing products derived from the kola nut.
Nervous system	The nervous system is the part of an animal's body that coordinates the actions of the animal and transmits signals between different parts of its body. In most types of animals it consists of two main parts, the central nervous system and the peripheral nervous system. The CNS contains the brain and spinal cord.
Side effect	In medicine, a side effect is an effect, whether therapeutic or adverse, that is secondary to the one intended; although the term is predominantly employed to describe adverse effects, it can also apply to beneficial, but unintended, consequences of the use of a drug. Occasionally, drugs are prescribed or procedures performed specifically for their side effects; in that case, said side effect ceases to be a side effect, and is now an intended effect. For instance, X-rays were historically (and are currently) used as an imaging technique; the discovery of their oncolytic capability led to their employ in radiotherapy (ablation of malignant tumours.
Pseudoephedrine	Pseudoephedrine is a sympathomimetic drug of the phenethylamine and amphetamine chemical classes. It is used as a nasal/sinus decongestant and stimulant, or as a wakefulness-promoting agent. The salts pseudoephedrine hydrochloride and pseudoephedrine sulfate are found in many over-the-counter preparations either as a single ingredient or, more commonly, in combination with antihistamines, guaifenesin, dextromethorphan, paracetamol (acetaminophen), and/or NSAIDs (e.g., aspirin, ibuprofen, etc)..

Methamphetamine	Methamphetamine, methylamphetamine, N-methylamphetamine, desoxyephedrine, and colloquially as 'meth' or 'crystal meth', is a psychostimulant of the phenethylamine and amphetamine class of drugs. It increases alertness, concentration, energy, and in high doses, can induce euphoria, enhance self-esteem, and increase libido. Methamphetamine has high potential for abuse and addiction by activating the psychological reward system via triggering a cascading release of dopamine, norepinephrine and serotonin in the brain.
Diphenhydramine	Diphenhydramine hydrochloride is a first generation antihistamine mainly used to treat allergies. Like most other first generation antihistamines, the drug also has a powerful hypnotic effect, and for this reason is often used as a nonprescription sleep aid and a mild anxiolytic. The drug also acts as an antiemetic.
Insomnia	Insomnia, is a sleep disorder in which there is an inability to fall asleep or to stay asleep as long as desired. While the term is sometimes used to describe a disorder demonstrated by polysomnographic evidence of disturbed sleep, insomnia is often practically defined as a positive response to either of two questions: 'Do you experience difficulty sleeping?' or 'Do you have difficulty falling or staying asleep?'

Thus, insomnia is most often thought of as both a sign and a symptom that can accompany several sleep, medical, and psychiatric disorders characterized by a persistent difficulty falling asleep and/or staying asleep or sleep of poor quality. Insomnia is typically followed by functional impairment while awake. |
| Amphetamine | Amphetamine or amfetamine (INN) is a psychostimulant drug of the phenethylamine class that is known to produce increased wakefulness and focus in association with decreased fatigue and appetite.

Brand names of medications that contain, or metabolize into, amphetamine include Adderall, Dexedrine, Dextrostat, Desoxyn, ProCentra, and Vyvanse, as well as Benzedrine in the past.

The drug is also used recreationally and as a performance enhancer. |
| Depressant | A depressant, is a drug or endogenous compound that lowers or depresses arousal levels and reduces excitability. Depressants are also occasionally referred to as 'downers' as they lower the level of arousal when taken. Stimulants or 'uppers' increase mental and/or physical function are the functional opposites of depressants. |
| Dextromethorphan | Dextromethorphan is an antitussive (cough suppressant) drug. It is one of the active ingredients in many over-the-counter cold and cough medicines, such as Robitussin, NyQuil, Dimetapp, Vicks, Coricidin, Delsym, and others, including generic labels. |

Chapter 14. Over-the-Counter, Prescription, and Herbal Drugs

Stimulant	Stimulants (also called psychostimulants) are psychoactive drugs which induce temporary improvements in either mental or physical function or both. Examples of these kinds of effects may include enhanced alertness, wakefulness, and locomotion, among others. Due to their effects typically having an 'up' quality to them, stimulants are also occasionally referred to as 'uppers'.
Drug interaction	A drug interaction is a situation in which a substance affects the activity of a drug, i.e. the effects are increased or decreased, or they produce a new effect that neither produces on its own. Typically, interaction between drugs come to mind (drug-drug interaction). However, interactions may also exist between drugs & foods (drug-food interactions), as well as drugs & herbs (drug-herb interactions).
Toxicity	Toxicity is the degree to which a substance can damage an organism. Toxicity can refer to the effect on a whole organism, such as an animal, bacterium, or plant, as well as the effect on a substructure of the organism, such as a cell (cytotoxicity) or an organ (organotoxicity), such as the liver (hepatotoxicity). By extension, the word may be metaphorically used to describe toxic effects on larger and more complex groups, such as the family unit or society at large.
Antidepressant	Antidepressants, despite their name, are often used to treat other conditions, on- or off-label, for conditions such as anxiety disorders, obsessive compulsive disorder, eating disorders, chronic pain, and some hormone-mediated disorders such as dysmenorrhea, and for snoring, migraines, attention-deficit hyperactivity disorder, (ADHD) substance abuse and occasionally even insomnia. Antidepressants are used either alone or combination with other medications. Most antidepressants have a delayed onset of action (2-6 weeks) but for responders, efficacy is often seen after one week.
Depression	Depression is a state of low mood and aversion to activity that can affect a person's thoughts, behavior, feelings and physical well-being. Depressed people may feel sad, anxious, empty, hopeless, worried, helpless, worthless, guilty, irritable, or restless. They may lose interest in activities that once were pleasurable; experience loss of appetite or overeating, have problems concentrating, remembering details, or making decisions; and may contemplate or attempt suicide.
Bronchodilator	A bronchodilator is a substance that dilates the bronchi and bronchioles, decreasing resistance in the respiratory airway and increasing airflow to the lungs. Bronchodilators may be endogenous (originating naturally within the body), or they may be medications administered for the treatment of breathing difficulties. They are most useful in obstructive lung diseases, of which asthma and chronic obstructive pulmonary disease are the most common conditions.
Edema	Edema, formerly known as dropsy or hydropsy, is an abnormal accumulation of fluid beneath the skin or in one or more cavities of the body.

Hypertension	Hypertension or high blood pressure, sometimes called arterial hypertension, is a chronic medical condition in which the blood pressure in the arteries is elevated. This requires the heart to work harder than normal to circulate blood through the blood vessels. Blood pressure is summarised by two measurements, systolic and diastolic, which depend on whether the heart muscle is contracting (systole) or relaxed between beats (diastole).
Cocaine	Cocaine benzoylmethylecgonine (INN) is a crystalline tropane alkaloid that is obtained from the leaves of the coca plant. The name comes from 'coca' in addition to the alkaloid suffix -ine, forming cocaine. It is a stimulant of the central nervous system, an appetite suppressant, and a topical anesthetic.
Adderall	Adderall is a brand-name psychostimulant medication composed of racemic amphetamine aspartate monohydrate, racemic amphetamine sulfate, dextroamphetamine saccharide, and dextroamphetamine sulfate, which is thought by scientists to work by increasing the amount of dopamine and norepinephrine in the brain. In addition, the drug also acts as a potent dopamine reuptake inhibitor and norepinephrine reuptake inhibitor. Adderall is widely reported to increase alertness, increase libido, increase concentration and overall cognitive performance, and, in general, improve mood, while decreasing user fatigue.
Hypothyroidism	Hypothyroidism is a deficiency of thyroid hormone in humans and other vertebrates. Iodine deficiency is the most common cause of hypothyroidism worldwide but it can be caused by any number of other causes such as several conditions of the the thyroid gland, or less commonly, the pituitary gland or hypothalamus. It can result from a lack of a thyroid gland.
Methylphenidate	Methylphenidate is a psychostimulant drug approved for treatment of attention-deficit hyperactivity disorder, postural orthostatic tachycardia syndrome, and narcolepsy. It may also be prescribed for off-label use in treatment-resistant cases of lethargy, depression, neural insult and obesity. Methylphenidate belongs to the piperidine class of compounds and increases the levels of dopamine and norepinephrine in the brain through reuptake inhibition of the monoamine transporters.
Anabolic steroid	Anabolic steroids, technically known as anabolic-androgen steroids, are drugs which mimic the effects of the male sex hormones testosterone and dihydrotestosterone. They increase protein synthesis within cells, which results in the buildup of cellular tissue (anabolism), especially in muscles. Anabolic steroids also have androgenic and virilizing properties, including the development and maintenance of masculine characteristics such as the growth of the vocal cords and body hair.
Crack cocaine	Crack cocaine is the freebase form of cocaine that can be smoked.

Chapter 14. Over-the-Counter, Prescription, and Herbal Drugs

It may also be termed rock, hard, iron, cavvy, base, or just crack.

Appearance and characteristics

In purer forms, crack rocks appear as off-white nuggets with jagged edges, with a slightly higher density than candle wax.

1. A _____ is a situation in which a substance affects the activity of a drug, i.e. the effects are increased or decreased, or they produce a new effect that neither produces on its own. Typically, interaction between drugs come to mind (drug-_____). However, interactions may also exist between drugs & foods (drug-food interactions), as well as drugs & herbs (drug-herb interactions).

    a. Drug interaction
    b. Becaplermin
    c. Biomed 101
    d. Biosimilar

2. _____ is a term used to describe drugs which are created (or marketed, if they had already existed) to get around existing drug laws, usually by modifying the molecular structures of existing drugs to varying degrees, or less commonly by finding drugs with entirely different chemical structures that produce similar subjective effects to illegal recreational drugs.

    History

    United States

    1920s-1930s

    The term '_____' was first coined by law enforcement in the 1980s, and has gained widespread use. However the first appearance of what would now be termed _____s occurred well before this, in the 1920s.

    a. Form constant
    b. Designer drug
    c. Hallucination
    d. Hallucinogen persisting perception disorder

3. _____ or amfetamine (INN) is a psychostimulant drug of the phenethylamine class that is known to produce increased wakefulness and focus in association with decreased fatigue and appetite.

Brand names of medications that contain, or metabolize into, _____ include Adderall, Dexedrine, Dextrostat, Desoxyn, ProCentra, and Vyvanse, as well as Benzedrine in the past.

The drug is also used recreationally and as a performance enhancer.

a. Aplindore
b. Amphetamine
c. Azapride
d. Etilevodopa

4. _____ is a bitter, white crystalline xanthine alkaloid that acts as a stimulant drug. _____ is found in varying quantities in the seeds, leaves, and fruit of some plants, where it acts as a natural pesticide that paralyzes and kills certain insects feeding on the plants. It is most commonly consumed by humans in infusions extracted from the seed of the coffee plant and the leaves of the tea bush, as well as from various foods and drinks containing products derived from the kola nut.

a. Caffeine
b. CCK-4
c. Meta-Chlorophenylpiperazine
d. Cholecystokinin

5. _____ is a sympathomimetic drug of the phenethylamine and amphetamine chemical classes. It is used as a nasal/sinus decongestant and stimulant, or as a wakefulness-promoting agent. The salts _____ hydrochloride and _____ sulfate are found in many over-the-counter preparations either as a single ingredient or, more commonly, in combination with antihistamines, guaifenesin, dextromethorphan, paracetamol (acetaminophen), and/or NSAIDs (e.g., aspirin, ibuprofen, etc)..

a. Pseudoephedrine
b. mechanism of action
c. Benzoylecgonine
d. Therapeutic index

1. a
2. b
3. b
4. a
5. a

You can take the complete Chapter Practice Test

for Chapter 14. Over-the-Counter, Prescription, and Herbal Drugs
on all key terms, persons, places, and concepts.

Online 99 Cents

http://www.epub52.21.20957.14.cram101.com/

Use www.Cram101.com for all your study needs

including Cram101's online interactive problem solving labs in

chemistry, statistics, mathematics, and more.

Chapter 15. Drug Use in Subcultures of Special Populations

CHAPTER OUTLINE: KEY TERMS, PEOPLE, PLACES, CONCEPTS

Anabolic steroid

Demographic profile

Sexual abuse

Aggression

Intervention

Designer drug

Drug interaction

Stimulant

Amphetamine

Clenbuterol

Growth hormone

Alcoholics Anonymous

Higher Ground

Heroin

Domestic violence

Physical abuse

Fetal alcohol syndrome

Tobacco

Peer group

Chapter 15. Drug Use in Subcultures of Special Populations

CHAPTER OUTLINE: KEY TERMS, PEOPLE, PLACES, CONCEPTS

	Adolescence
	Sexual violence
	Suicide intervention
	Sexual assault
	Nervous system
	Acquaintance rape
	Dextropropoxyphene
	Crack cocaine
	Alcohol advertising

CHAPTER HIGHLIGHTS & NOTES: KEY TERMS, PEOPLE, PLACES, CONCEPTS

Anabolic steroid	Anabolic steroids, technically known as anabolic-androgen steroids, are drugs which mimic the effects of the male sex hormones testosterone and dihydrotestosterone. They increase protein synthesis within cells, which results in the buildup of cellular tissue (anabolism), especially in muscles. Anabolic steroids also have androgenic and virilizing properties, including the development and maintenance of masculine characteristics such as the growth of the vocal cords and body hair.
Demographic profile	A demographic profile is a term used in marketing and broadcasting, to describe a demographic grouping or a market segment. This typically involves age bands (as teenagers do not wish to purchase denture fixant), social class bands (as the rich may want different products than middle and lower classes and may be willing to pay more) and gender (partially because different physical attributes require different hygiene and clothing products, and partially because of the male/female mindsets).

Chapter 15. Drug Use in Subcultures of Special Populations

Sexual abuse	Sexual abuse, also referred to as molestation, is the forcing of undesired sexual behavior by one person upon another. When that force is immediate, of short duration, or infrequent, it is called sexual assault. The offender is referred to as a sexual abuser or (often pejoratively) molester.
Aggression	Aggression, in its broadest sense, is behavior, or a disposition, that is forceful, hostile or attacking. It may occur either in retaliation or without provocation. In narrower definitions that are used in social sciences and behavioral sciences, aggression is an intention to cause harm or an act intended to increase relative social dominance.
Intervention	An intervention is an orchestrated attempt by one or many, people - usually family and friends - to get someone to seek professional help with an addiction or some kind of traumatic event or crisis, or other serious problem. The term intervention is most often used when the traumatic event involves addiction to drugs or other items. Intervention can also refer to the act of using a similar technique within a therapy session.
Designer drug	Designer drug is a term used to describe drugs which are created (or marketed, if they had already existed) to get around existing drug laws, usually by modifying the molecular structures of existing drugs to varying degrees, or less commonly by finding drugs with entirely different chemical structures that produce similar subjective effects to illegal recreational drugs. History United States 1920s-1930s The term 'designer drug' was first coined by law enforcement in the 1980s, and has gained widespread use. However the first appearance of what would now be termed designer drugs occurred well before this, in the 1920s.
Drug interaction	A drug interaction is a situation in which a substance affects the activity of a drug, i.e. the effects are increased or decreased, or they produce a new effect that neither produces on its own. Typically, interaction between drugs come to mind (drug-drug interaction). However, interactions may also exist between drugs & foods (drug-food interactions), as well as drugs & herbs (drug-herb interactions).
Stimulant	Stimulants (also called psychostimulants) are psychoactive drugs which induce temporary improvements in either mental or physical function or both. Examples of these kinds of effects may include enhanced alertness, wakefulness, and locomotion, among others.

Chapter 15. Drug Use in Subcultures of Special Populations

Amphetamine	Amphetamine or amfetamine (INN) is a psychostimulant drug of the phenethylamine class that is known to produce increased wakefulness and focus in association with decreased fatigue and appetite.
	Brand names of medications that contain, or metabolize into, amphetamine include Adderall, Dexedrine, Dextrostat, Desoxyn, ProCentra, and Vyvanse, as well as Benzedrine in the past.
	The drug is also used recreationally and as a performance enhancer.
Clenbuterol	Clenbuterol is a sympathomimetic amine used by sufferers of breathing disorders as a decongestant and bronchodilator. People with chronic breathing disorders such as asthma use this as a bronchodilator to make breathing easier. It is most commonly available as the hydrochloride salt clenbuterol hydrochloride.
Growth hormone	Growth hormone is a protein-based peptide hormone. It stimulates growth, cell reproduction and regeneration in humans and other animals. Growth hormone is a 191-amino acid, single-chain polypeptide that is synthesized, stored, and secreted by the somatotroph cells within the lateral wings of the anterior pituitary gland.
Alcoholics Anonymous	Alcoholics Anonymous is an international mutual aid movement founded in 1935 by Bill Wilson and Dr. Bob Smith (Bill W. and Dr. Bob) in Akron, Ohio. AA states that its 'primary purpose is to stay sober and help other alcoholics achieve sobriety'. With other early members, Wilson and Smith developed AA's Twelve Step program of spiritual and character development.
Higher Ground	Higher Ground is a 501(C)3 HIV-AIDS non-profit support group based in Royal Oak, Michigan. Founded in 2002, it primarily serves metropolitan Detroit and southeastern Michigan. It frequently receives media coverage for public service.
Heroin	Heroin (diacetylmorphine (INN)), also known as diamorphine (BAN), is a semi-synthetic opioid drug synthesized from morphine, a derivative of the opium poppy. It is the 3,6-diacetyl ester of morphine (di (two)-acetyl-morphine). The white crystalline form is commonly the hydrochloride salt diacetylmorphine hydrochloride, though often adulterated thus dulling the sheen and consistency from that to a matte white powder, which diacetylmorphine freebase typically is. 90% of diacetylmorphine is thought to be produced in Afghanistan.
Domestic violence	Domestic violence, spousal abuse, battering, family violence, and intimate partner violence (IPV), is defined as a pattern of abusive behaviors by one partner against another in an intimate relationship such as marriage, dating, family, or cohabitation.

Domestic violence, so defined, has many forms, including physical aggression or assault (hitting, kicking, biting, shoving, restraining, slapping, throwing objects), or threats thereof; sexual abuse; emotional abuse; controlling or domineering; intimidation; stalking; passive/covert abuse (e.g., neglect); and economic deprivation.

Alcohol consumption and mental illness can be co-morbid with abuse, and present additional challenges in eliminating domestic violence.

Physical abuse	Physical abuse is an act of another party involving contact intended to cause feelings of physical pain, injury, or other physical suffering or bodily harm. Physical abuse has been described among animals too, for example among the Adélie penguins. In most cases, children are the victims of physical abuse, but adults can be the sufferers too.
Fetal alcohol syndrome	Fetal alcohol syndrome is a pattern of mental and physical defects that can develop in a fetus in association with high levels of alcohol consumption during pregnancy. Current research also implicates other lifestyle choices made by the prospective mother. Indications for lower levels of alcohol are inconclusive.
Tobacco	Tobacco is an agricultural product processed from the leaves of plants in the genus Nicotiana. It can be consumed, used as an organic pesticide and, in the form of nicotine tartrate, used in some medicines. It is most commonly used as a recreational drug, and is a valuable cash crop for countries such as Cuba, China and the United States.
Peer group	A peer group is a social group consisting of people. Peer groups are an informal primary group of people who share a similar or equal status and who are usually of roughly the same age, tended to travel around and interact within the social aggregate Members of a particular peer group often have similar interests and backgrounds, bonded by the premise of sameness. However, some peer groups are very diverse, crossing social divides such as socioeconomic status, level of education, race, creed, culture, or religion.
Adolescence	Adolescence is a transitional stage of physical and psychological human development generally occurring during the period from puberty to legal adulthood (age of majority). The period of adolescence is most closely associated with the teenage years, although its physical, psychological and cultural expressions can begin earlier and end later. For example, although puberty has been historically associated with the onset of adolescent development, it now typically begins prior to the teenage years and there has been a normative shift of it occurring in preadolescence, particularly in females .
Sexual violence	Sexual violence occurs throughout the world, although in most countries there has been little research conducted on the problem. Due to the private nature of sexual violence, estimating the extent of the problem is difficult.

Suicide intervention	Suicide intervention is a direct effort to prevent person(s) from attempting to take their own life intentionally. In the United States, individuals who express the intent to harm themselves are automatically determined to lack the present mental capacity to refuse treatment, and can be transported to an emergency department against their will. An emergency physician there will determine whether or not inpatient care at a mental health care facility is warranted.
Sexual assault	Sexual assault is an assault of a sexual nature on another person, or any sexual act committed without consent. Although sexual assaults most frequently are by a man on a woman, it may involve any combination of two or more men, women and children. The term sexual assault is used, in public discourse, as a generic term that is defined as any involuntary sexual act in which a person is threatened, coerced, or forced to engage against their will, or any sexual touching of a person who has not consented.
Nervous system	The nervous system is the part of an animal's body that coordinates the actions of the animal and transmits signals between different parts of its body. In most types of animals it consists of two main parts, the central nervous system and the peripheral nervous system. The CNS contains the brain and spinal cord.
Acquaintance rape	Acquaintance rape is an assault or attempted assault usually committed by a new acquaintance involving sexual intercourse without mutual consent. The term 'date rape' is widely used but can be misleading because the person who commits the crime might not be dating the victim. Rather, it could be an acquaintance or stranger.
Dextropropoxyphene	Dextropropoxyphene, manufactured by Eli Lilly and Company, is an analgesic in the opioid category. It is intended to to treat mild pain and has, in addition, anti-tussive and local anesthetic effects. It has been taken off the marked in Europe and the US due to concerns of fatal overdoses and arrhythmias.
Crack cocaine	Crack cocaine is the freebase form of cocaine that can be smoked. It may also be termed rock, hard, iron, cavvy, base, or just crack. Appearance and characteristics In purer forms, crack rocks appear as off-white nuggets with jagged edges, with a slightly higher density than candle wax.

Chapter 15. Drug Use in Subcultures of Special Populations

Alcohol advertising	Alcohol advertising is the promotion of alcoholic beverages by alcohol producers through a variety of media. Along with tobacco advertising, it is one of the most highly-regulated forms of marketing. Some or all forms of alcohol advertising is banned in some countries.

CHAPTER QUIZ: KEY TERMS, PEOPLE, PLACES, CONCEPTS

1. An _____ is an orchestrated attempt by one or many, people - usually family and friends - to get someone to seek professional help with an addiction or some kind of traumatic event or crisis, or other serious problem. The term _____ is most often used when the traumatic event involves addiction to drugs or other items. _____ can also refer to the act of using a similar technique within a therapy session.

    a. Online counseling
    b. Intervention
    c. United to End Racism
    d. Online deliberation

2. _____s (also called psycho_____s) are psychoactive drugs which induce temporary improvements in either mental or physical function or both. Examples of these kinds of effects may include enhanced alertness, wakefulness, and locomotion, among others. Due to their effects typically having an 'up' quality to them, _____s are also occasionally referred to as 'uppers'.

    a. Stimulant
    b. Vayarin
    c. Delivered from Distraction
    d. Functional disconnection

3. _____ (diacetylmorphine (INN)), also known as diamorphine (BAN), is a semi-synthetic opioid drug synthesized from morphine, a derivative of the opium poppy. It is the 3,6-diacetyl ester of morphine (di (two)-acetyl-morphine). The white crystalline form is commonly the hydrochloride salt diacetylmorphine hydrochloride, though often adulterated thus dulling the sheen and consistency from that to a matte white powder, which diacetylmorphine freebase typically is. 90% of diacetylmorphine is thought to be produced in Afghanistan.

    a. Heroin
    b. Pethidine
    c. Loperamide
    d. Posse Comitatus Act

4. . _____, also referred to as molestation, is the forcing of undesired sexual behavior by one person upon another.

When that force is immediate, of short duration, or infrequent, it is called sexual assault. The offender is referred to as a sexual abuser or (often pejoratively) molester.

a. Sexual abuse
b. The Survivors Trust
c. Whipping Tom
d. National Sexual Violence Resource Center

5. _____s, technically known as anabolic-androgen steroids, are drugs which mimic the effects of the male sex hormones testosterone and dihydrotestosterone. They increase protein synthesis within cells, which results in the buildup of cellular tissue (anabolism), especially in muscles. _____s also have androgenic and virilizing properties, including the development and maintenance of masculine characteristics such as the growth of the vocal cords and body hair.

a. Immanuel Kant
b. Organized Crime Control Act
c. Anabolic steroid
d. Abnormal psychology

1. b
2. a
3. a
4. a
5. c

You can take the complete Chapter Practice Test

for Chapter 15. Drug Use in Subcultures of Special Populations
on all key terms, persons, places, and concepts.

Online 99 Cents

http://www.epub52.21.20957.15.cram101.com/

Use www.Cram101.com for all your study needs

including Cram101's online interactive problem solving labs in

chemistry, statistics, mathematics, and more.

Chapter 16. Drug Abuse Prevention

CHAPTER OUTLINE: KEY TERMS, PEOPLE, PLACES, CONCEPTS

_____ Higher Ground

_____ Prevalence

_____ Protective factor

_____ Harm reduction

_____ Drug education

_____ Attitude change

_____ Nervous system

_____ Social influence

_____ Axon

_____ Peer group

_____ Neuron

_____ Heroin

_____ Drug court

_____ Alcoholics Anonymous

_____ Stimulant

Higher Ground	Higher Ground is a 501(C)3 HIV-AIDS non-profit support group based in Royal Oak, Michigan. Founded in 2002, it primarily serves metropolitan Detroit and southeastern Michigan. It frequently receives media coverage for public service.
Prevalence	In epidemiology, the prevalence of a health-related state (typically disease, but also other things like smoking or seatbelt use) in a statistical population is defined as the total number of cases of the risk factor in the population at a given time, or the total number of cases in the population, divided by the number of individuals in the population. It is used as an estimate of how common a disease is within a population over a certain period of time. It helps physicians or other health professionals understand the probability of certain diagnoses and is routinely used by epidemiologists, health care providers, government agencies and insurers.
Protective factor	Protective factors are conditions or attributes (skills, strengths, resources, supports or coping strategies) in individuals, families, communities or the larger society that help people deal more effectively with stressful events and mitigate or eliminate risk in families and communities.
	Protective factors include:•Adoptive parents having an accurate understanding of their adopted children's pre-adoption medical and behavioral problems •Assistance of adoption professionals in the home of adopted children
	Some risks that adopted children are prone to :•Self-mutilation•Delinquency•Trouble with the law•Substance abuse•Thievery.
Harm reduction	Harm reduction refers to a range of public health policies designed to reduce the harmful consequences associated with human behaviors, even if those behaviors are risky or illegal. Examples of behaviors targeted for harm reduction policies include recreational drug use and prostitution. Criticism of harm reduction typically centers on concerns that tolerating risky or illegal behaviour sends a message to the community that these behaviours are acceptable.
Drug education	Drug education is the planned provision of information and skills relevant to living in a world where drugs are commonly misused. Planning includes developing strategies for helping children and young people engage with relevant drug-related issues during opportunistic and brief contacts with them as well as during more structured sessions. Drug education enables children and young adults to develop the knowledge, skills and attitudes to appreciate the benefits of a healthy lifestyle, promote responsibility towards the use of drugs and relate these to their own actions and those of others, both now and in their future lives. It also provides opportunities for young people to reflect on their own and others' attitudes to drugs, drug usage and drug users.
Attitude change	Attitudes are the evaluations and associated beliefs and behaviors towards some object.

Chapter 16. Drug Abuse Prevention

They are not stable, and because of the communication and behavior of other people, are subject to change by social influences, as well as an individual's motivation to maintain cognitive consistency when cognitive dissonance occurs--when two attitudes or when attitude and behavior conflict. Attitudes and attitude objects are functions of affective and cognitive components. It has been suggested that the inter-structural composition of an associative network can be altered by the activation of a single node. Thus, by activating an affective or emotion node, attitude change may be possible, though affective and cognitive components tend to be intertwined.

Nervous system	The nervous system is the part of an animal's body that coordinates the actions of the animal and transmits signals between different parts of its body. In most types of animals it consists of two main parts, the central nervous system and the peripheral nervous system. The CNS contains the brain and spinal cord.
Social influence	Social influence occurs when one's emotions, opinions, or behaviors are affected by others. Social influence takes many forms and can be seen in conformity, socialization, peer pressure, obedience, leadership, persuaon, sales, and marketing. In 1958, Harvard psychologist, Herbert Kelman identified three broad varieties of social influence.
Axon	An axon also known as a nerve fibre; is a long, slender projection of a nerve cell, or neuron, that typically conducts electrical impulses away from the neuron's cell body. The function of the axon is to transmit information to different neurons, muscles and glands. In certain sensory neurons (pseudounipolar neurons), such as those for touch and warmth, the electrical impulse travels along an axon from the periphery to the cell body, and from the cell body to the spinal cord along another branch of the same axon.
Peer group	A peer group is a social group consisting of people. Peer groups are an informal primary group of people who share a similar or equal status and who are usually of roughly the same age, tended to travel around and interact within the social aggregate Members of a particular peer group often have similar interests and backgrounds, bonded by the premise of sameness. However, some peer groups are very diverse, crossing social divides such as socioeconomic status, level of education, race, creed, culture, or religion.
Neuron	A neuron is an electrically excitable cell that processes and transmits information by electrical and chemical signaling. Chemical signaling occurs via synapses, specialized connections with other cells. Neurons connect to each other to form networks. Neurons are the core components of the nervous system, which includes the brain, spinal cord, and peripheral ganglia. A number of specialized types of neurons exist: sensory neurons respond to touch, sound, light and numerous other stimuli affecting cells of the sensory organs that then send signals to the spinal cord and brain. Motor neurons receive signals from the brain and spinal cord, cause muscle contractions, and affect glands.

CHAPTER HIGHLIGHTS & NOTES: KEY TERMS, PEOPLE, PLACES, CONCEPTS

Heroin	Heroin (diacetylmorphine (INN)), also known as diamorphine (BAN), is a semi-synthetic opioid drug synthesized from morphine, a derivative of the opium poppy. It is the 3,6-diacetyl ester of morphine (di (two)-acetyl-morphine). The white crystalline form is commonly the hydrochloride salt diacetylmorphine hydrochloride, though often adulterated thus dulling the sheen and consistency from that to a matte white powder, which diacetylmorphine freebase typically is. 90% of diacetylmorphine is thought to be produced in Afghanistan.
Drug court	Drug Courts are judicially supervised court dockets that handle the cases of nonviolent substance abusing offenders under the adult, juvenile, family and tribal justice systems. Drug Courts operate under a specialized model in which the judiciary, prosecution, defense bar, probation, law enforcement, mental health, social service, and treatment communities work together to help non-violent offenders find restoration in recovery and become productive citizens. In the USA, there are currently over 2,459 Drug Courts representing all fifty states.
Alcoholics Anonymous	Alcoholics Anonymous is an international mutual aid movement founded in 1935 by Bill Wilson and Dr. Bob Smith (Bill W. and Dr. Bob) in Akron, Ohio. AA states that its 'primary purpose is to stay sober and help other alcoholics achieve sobriety'. With other early members, Wilson and Smith developed AA's Twelve Step program of spiritual and character development.
Stimulant	Stimulants (also called psychostimulants) are psychoactive drugs which induce temporary improvements in either mental or physical function or both. Examples of these kinds of effects may include enhanced alertness, wakefulness, and locomotion, among others. Due to their effects typically having an 'up' quality to them, stimulants are also occasionally referred to as 'uppers'.

CHAPTER QUIZ: KEY TERMS, PEOPLE, PLACES, CONCEPTS

1. A _____ is a social group consisting of people. _____s are an informal primary group of people who share a similar or equal status and who are usually of roughly the same age, tended to travel around and interact within the social aggregate Members of a particular _____ often have similar interests and backgrounds, bonded by the premise of sameness. However, some _____s are very diverse, crossing social divides such as socioeconomic status, level of education, race, creed, culture, or religion.

    a. Household
    b. Posse Comitatus Act
    c. Peer group
    d. Electroencephalography

2. . _____ is a 501(C)3 HIV-AIDS non-profit support group based in Royal Oak, Michigan.

Chapter 16. Drug Abuse Prevention

Founded in 2002, it primarily serves metropolitan Detroit and southeastern Michigan. It frequently receives media coverage for public service.

a. Higher Ground
b. Hoffman Institute
c. Holland Codes
d. Initial Professional Development

3. A _____ is an electrically excitable cell that processes and transmits information by electrical and chemical signaling. Chemical signaling occurs via synapses, specialized connections with other cells. _____s connect to each other to form networks. _____s are the core components of the nervous system, which includes the brain, spinal cord, and peripheral ganglia. A number of specialized types of _____s exist: sensory _____s respond to touch, sound, light and numerous other stimuli affecting cells of the sensory organs that then send signals to the spinal cord and brain. Motor _____s receive signals from the brain and spinal cord, cause muscle contractions, and affect glands. Inter_____s connect _____s to other _____s within the same region of the brain or spinal cord.

a. Past medical history
b. Neuron
c. Posse Comitatus Act
d. Electroencephalography

4. _____s are judicially supervised court dockets that handle the cases of nonviolent substance abusing offenders under the adult, juvenile, family and tribal justice systems. _____s operate under a specialized model in which the judiciary, prosecution, defense bar, probation, law enforcement, mental health, social service, and treatment communities work together to help non-violent offenders find restoration in recovery and become productive citizens. In the USA, there are currently over 2,459 _____s representing all fifty states.

a. Drug detoxification
b. Givat Shemesh
c. Drug court
d. Higher Power

5. . In epidemiology, the _____ of a health-related state (typically disease, but also other things like smoking or seatbelt use) in a statistical population is defined as the total number of cases of the risk factor in the population at a given time, or the total number of cases in the population, divided by the number of individuals in the population. It is used as an estimate of how common a disease is within a population over a certain period of time. It helps physicians or other health professionals understand the probability of certain diagnoses and is routinely used by epidemiologists, health care providers, government agencies and insurers.

a. Preventive fraction
b. ProMED-mail
c. Propensity score matching

ANSWER KEY
Chapter 16. Drug Abuse Prevention

1. c
2. a
3. b
4. c
5. d

You can take the complete Chapter Practice Test

for Chapter 16. Drug Abuse Prevention
on all key terms, persons, places, and concepts.

Online 99 Cents

http://www.epub52.21.20957.16.cram101.com/

Use www.Cram101.com for all your study needs

including Cram101's online interactive problem solving labs in

chemistry, statistics, mathematics, and more.

_____ | Alcoholics Anonymous

_____ | Comorbidity

_____ | Mental disorder

_____ | Salvia divinorum

_____ | Schizophrenia

_____ | Heroin

_____ | Therapeutic community

_____ | Motivational Enhancement Therapy

_____ | Methadone

_____ | Naltrexone

_____ | Partial agonist

_____ | Acamprosate

_____ | Drug interaction

_____ | Psychosocial

Chapter 17. Treating Drug Dependence

Alcoholics Anonymous	Alcoholics Anonymous is an international mutual aid movement founded in 1935 by Bill Wilson and Dr. Bob Smith (Bill W. and Dr. Bob) in Akron, Ohio. AA states that its 'primary purpose is to stay sober and help other alcoholics achieve sobriety'. With other early members, Wilson and Smith developed AA's Twelve Step program of spiritual and character development.
Comorbidity	In medicine, comorbidity is either the presence of one or more disorders in addition to a primary disease or disorder, or the effect of such additional disorders or diseases. In medicine In medicine, comorbidity describes the effect of all other diseases an individual patient might have other than the primary disease of interest. Many tests attempt to standardize the 'weight' or value of comorbid conditions, whether they are secondary or tertiary illnesses.
Mental disorder	A mental disorder is a psychological pattern or anomaly, potentially reflected in behavior, that is generally associated with distress or disability, and which is not considered part of normal development of a person's culture. Mental disorders are generally defined by a combination of how a person feels, acts, thinks or perceives. This may be associated with particular regions or functions of the brain or rest of the nervous system, often in a social context.
Salvia divinorum	Salvia divinorum is a psychoactive plant which can induce dissociative effects and is a potent producer of 'visions' and other hallucinatory experiences. Its native habitat is within cloud forest in the isolated Sierra Mazateca of Oaxaca, Mexico, where it grows in shady and moist locations. The plant grows to over a meter high, has hollow square stems, large leaves, and occasional white flowers with violet calyxes.
Schizophrenia	Schizophrenia is a mental disorder characterized by a disintegration of thought processes and of emotional responsiveness. It most commonly manifests as auditory hallucinations, paranoid or bizarre delusions, or disorganized speech and thinking, and it is accompanied by significant social or occupational dysfunction. The onset of symptoms typically occurs in young adulthood, with a global lifetime prevalence of about 0.3-0.7%.
Heroin	Heroin (diacetylmorphine (INN)), also known as diamorphine (BAN), is a semi-synthetic opioid drug synthesized from morphine, a derivative of the opium poppy. It is the 3,6-diacetyl ester of morphine (di (two)-acetyl-morphine). The white crystalline form is commonly the hydrochloride salt diacetylmorphine hydrochloride, though often adulterated thus dulling the sheen and consistency from that to a matte white powder, which diacetylmorphine freebase typically is. 90% of diacetylmorphine is thought to be produced in Afghanistan.
Therapeutic community	Therapeutic community is a term applied to a participative, group-based approach to long-term mental illness, personality disorders and drug addiction.

The approach is usually residential with the clients and therapists living together, is based on milieu therapy principles and includes group psychotherapy as well as practical activities.

Therapeutic communities have gained some reputation for success in rehabilitation and patient satisfaction in Britain and abroad. In Britain, 'democratic analytic' therapeutic communities have tended to specialise in the treatment of moderate to severe personality disorders and complex emotional and interpersonal problems. The evolution of therapeutic communities in the United States has followed a different path with hierarchically arranged communities (or concept houses) specialising in the treatment of drug and alcohol dependence.

Motivational Enhancement Therapy	Motivational Enhancement Therapy is a time-limited four-session adaptation used in Project MATCH, a US-government-funded study of treatment for alcohol problems and the Drinkers' Check-up, which provides normative-based feedback and explores client motivation to change in light of the feedback. It is a development of Motivational Interviewing and Motivational therapy.
Methadone	Methadone is a synthetic opioid, used medically as an analgesic and a maintenance anti-addictive for use in patients on opioids. It was developed in Germany in 1937. Although chemically unlike morphine or heroin, methadone also acts on the opioid receptors and thus produces many of the same effects. Methadone is also used in managing chronic pain owing to its long duration of action and very low cost.
Naltrexone	Naltrexone is an opioid receptor antagonist used primarily in the management of alcohol dependence and opioid dependence. It is marketed in generic form as its hydrochloride salt, naltrexone hydrochloride, and marketed under the trade names Revia and Depade. In some countries including the United States, a once-monthly extended-release injectable formulation is marketed under the trade name Vivitrol.
Partial agonist	In pharmacology, partial agonists are drugs that bind to and activate a given receptor, but have only partial efficacy at the receptor relative to a full agonist. They may also be considered ligands which display both agonistic and antagonistic effects - when both a full agonist and partial agonist are present, the partial agonist actually acts as a competitive antagonist, competing with the full agonist for receptor occupancy and producing a net decrease in the receptor activation observed with the full agonist alone. Clinically, partial agonists can be used to activate receptors to give a desired submaximal response when inadequate amounts of the endogenous ligand are present, or they can reduce the overstimulation of receptors when excess amounts of the endogenous ligand are present.
Acamprosate	Acamprosate, is a drug used for treating alcohol dependence.

Chapter 17. Treating Drug Dependence

	Acamprosate is thought to stabilize the chemical balance in the brain that would otherwise be disrupted by alcoholism, possibly by antagonizing glutamatergic N-methyl-D-aspartate receptors and agonizing gamma-aminobutyric acid (GABA) type A receptors. Reports indicate that acamprosate only works with a combination of attending support groups and abstinence from alcohol.
Drug interaction	A drug interaction is a situation in which a substance affects the activity of a drug, i.e. the effects are increased or decreased, or they produce a new effect that neither produces on its own. Typically, interaction between drugs come to mind (drug-drug interaction). However, interactions may also exist between drugs & foods (drug-food interactions), as well as drugs & herbs (drug-herb interactions).
Psychosocial	For a concept to be psychosocial means it relates to one's psychological development in, and interaction with, a social environment. The individual needs not be fully aware of this relationship with his or her environment. It was first commonly used by psychologist Erik Erikson in his stages of social development.

1. _____ is a psychoactive plant which can induce dissociative effects and is a potent producer of 'visions' and other hallucinatory experiences. Its native habitat is within cloud forest in the isolated Sierra Mazateca of Oaxaca, Mexico, where it grows in shady and moist locations. The plant grows to over a meter high, has hollow square stems, large leaves, and occasional white flowers with violet calyxes.

    a. Serenic
    b. Salvia divinorum
    c. Sulfozinum
    d. Theanine

2. A _____ is a situation in which a substance affects the activity of a drug, i.e. the effects are increased or decreased, or they produce a new effect that neither produces on its own. Typically, interaction between drugs come to mind (drug-_____). However, interactions may also exist between drugs & foods (drug-food interactions), as well as drugs & herbs (drug-herb interactions).

    a. Drug interaction
    b. Becaplermin
    c. Biomed 101
    d. Biosimilar

Chapter 17. Treating Drug Dependence

3. _____ is an international mutual aid movement founded in 1935 by Bill Wilson and Dr. Bob Smith (Bill W. and Dr. Bob) in Akron, Ohio. AA states that its 'primary purpose is to stay sober and help other alcoholics achieve sobriety'. With other early members, Wilson and Smith developed AA's Twelve Step program of spiritual and character development.

   a. Higher Power
   b. Alcoholics Anonymous
   c. Keeley Institute
   d. Tired and emotional

4. _____ is a term applied to a participative, group-based approach to long-term mental illness, personality disorders and drug addiction. The approach is usually residential with the clients and therapists living together, is based on milieu therapy principles and includes group psychotherapy as well as practical activities.

   _____(ies) have gained some reputation for success in rehabilitation and patient satisfaction in Britain and abroad. In Britain, 'democratic analytic' _____(ies) have tended to specialise in the treatment of moderate to severe personality disorders and complex emotional and interpersonal problems. The evolution of _____(ies) in the United States has followed a different path with hierarchically arranged communities (or concept houses) specialising in the treatment of drug and alcohol dependence.

   a. Therapeutic community
   b. Social Therapy
   c. Behavior modification facility
   d. Bili light

5. In medicine, _____ is either the presence of one or more disorders in addition to a primary disease or disorder, or the effect of such additional disorders or diseases. In medicine

   In medicine, _____ describes the effect of all other diseases an individual patient might have other than the primary disease of interest.

   Many tests attempt to standardize the 'weight' or value of comorbid conditions, whether they are secondary or tertiary illnesses.

   a. Comorbidity
   b. Hallucinogen persisting perception disorder
   c. National Mental Health Anti-Stigma Campaign
   d. Neuroleptic malignant syndrome

1. b
2. a
3. b
4. a
5. a

You can take the complete Chapter Practice Test

for Chapter 17. Treating Drug Dependence
on all key terms, persons, places, and concepts.

Online 99 Cents

http://www.epub52.21.20957.17.cram101.com/

Use www.Cram101.com for all your study needs
including Cram101's online interactive problem solving labs in
chemistry, statistics, mathematics, and more.

Other Cram101 e-Books and Tests

Want More?
Cram101.com...

Cram101.com provides the outlines and highlights of your textbooks, just like this e-StudyGuide, but also gives you the PRACTICE TESTS, and other exclusive study tools for all of your textbooks.

Learn More. *Just click*
http://www.cram101.com/

CPSIA information can be obtained at www.ICGtesting.com
Printed in the USA
LVOW09s1421200114

370183LV00001B/13/P